MAKE
IT FIT

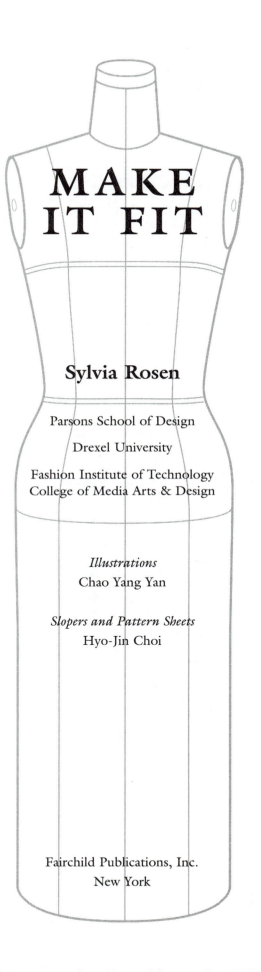

MAKE IT FIT

Sylvia Rosen

Parsons School of Design

Drexel University

Fashion Institute of Technology
College of Media Arts & Design

Illustrations
Chao Yang Yan

Slopers and Pattern Sheets
Hyo-Jin Choi

Fairchild Publications, Inc.
New York

Executive Editor: Olga T. Kontzias
Assistant Acquisitions Editor: Jason Moring
Associate Production Editor: Elizabeth Marotta
Art Director: Adam B. Bohannon
Director of Production: Priscilla Taguer
Editorial Assistant: Suzette Lam
Publishing Assistant: Jaclyn Bergeron
Copy Editor: Amy Jolin
Interior Design: Susan C. Day
Cover Design: Adam B. Bohannon
Cover Photos of the author and Hyo-Jin Choi
by Seichi Tsutsumi

Library of Congress Catalog Card Number:
2004101106

ISBN:
1-56367-339-8

GST R 133004424

Printed in the United States of America

Contents

Preface

What Is a Pattern?

A pattern, for the dress form or the human body, is a blueprint, an outline, or a template to create a shape. Patterns create all of the components needed to form a complete unit of clothing. All patterns, regardless of size or shape, include important markings necessary to fit the pieces together precisely. They also give information to the sewer as to which pieces are sewn together and the sewing sequence.

What Is a Sloper?

All garments and designs are developed from patterns that are referred to as slopers, master patterns, foundations, blocks, or basic patterns.

Every company develops its own specifications and measurements that are adapted from government specifications, which are evaluated every seven years. They are based on the statistics compiled to fit the majority of people. Companies adapt these statistics to create and determine their own fit and look. As a result, no two firms will have the same fit, since no two companies use precisely the same measurements.

All slopers, after being adjusted, go through the process of being trued and checked for fit, balance, and accuracy before being used for pattern and style development.

The slopers in this *Make It Fit* kit have minimum ease and seam allowances added on, so as to have room and be able to adjust, increase, or decrease various areas shown on the diagrams in each chapter.

After the slopers are adjusted to fit the measurements needed for the form or the human body, each sloper should be trued carefully and traced to oak tag. Seam allowances are usually *not* added to these slopers, as the seams would interfere with pattern design and development.

About the Printed Slopers

The slopers in this kit are printed on pellon, a non-woven fabric, and they are made to fit the Wolf Form Co., Size 8, 2001, dress form.

It is important to follow the diagrams in:

Chapter 2 – Take accurate measurements, Document
Chapter 4 – Adjust Your Slopers for Fit
Chapter 6 – Test Fit on Form or Body
Chapter 7 – Grading Chart

The measurements should be documented on the charts, with a + (plus) or − (minus) for establishing good basic fit for use on the dress forms or on a person.

All dress forms of the same size, year, or manufacturer are not created equally. Much like clothing they are made (sewn) by hand, and as a result there may be anywhere from ¼" to ½" variance in circumference (horizontal), and ¼" to ³⁄₁₆" in length (vertical) measurements. Like the human body, not all persons of the same size have precisely the same proportions or measurements, and yet they still fit into a size 8. One may be a thin 8, a medium 8, or a "fat" 8. So clothing, and therefore the slopers, will fit each one differently. Also, the printing process on the pellon may create a slight variance, ⅛" to ¼" in width or length.

By following the diagrams and instructions in the manual, measuring carefully, one should be able to create slopers that fit. Muslins may need to be fitted and adjusted more than once before a final perfect set of slopers are achieved. Please refer to the following section, Notes to Users.

Apparel Sizing

Ideal body proportions in the western world cannot be accepted as the standard because of the wide variety of figure types.

The history of pattern making can be traced back to the 16th century when patterns were used as a guide for tailors. The industry as we know it today began in 1854, when Ebenezer Butterick, a tailor, made a dress for his wife. Upon requests from friends, he graded the pattern and marketed the dress. This was the beginning of the American pattern industry. His competitor, in 1872, was James McCall, who arrived from Scotland with his wife and opened a tailor shop. In 1899, *Vogue*, a New York magazine, introduced patterns and in 1927 Simplicity joined the industry.

The American Society for Testing and Materials (ASTM), was created in 1898, as a nonprofit organization to assist American manufacturers in adapting voluntary uniform product standards.

The National Bureau of Standards (NBS) was created in 1901 by the federal government. Using statistics compiled from surveys of the population, the NBS developed its own sizing standards. The pattern industry, responding to consumer needs, then established its own measurement standard committee. Global trading and the percentage shift of our population have invalidated many of these standards.

Major mass merchandisers, such as J. C. Penney and Sears developed their own pattern specifications that became the standard for other manufacturers.

There has been a major shift of people (baby boomers, 76 million as of 1996) between the ages 45–65. The largest percentage are seniors over 65. Baby boomers turning 50 in 1996 will fall into the 55+ category in the next 20 years. Current statistics also show that obesity is now a world-wide epidemic, affecting all age groups and races.

Statistics based on the changing female figure is affecting the prototype of the "ideal" female figure. Fit and sizing specifications are changing to meet the needs of this new female figure with the plus size market category becoming increasingly important for manufacturers and designers.

Notes to User

Dress Form and Body Measurements

This *Make It Fit* kit include sets of one-half model slopers used as a basis for designing apparel. They are based on dress form Size 8, 2001, Wolf Form Co. measurements. The slopers all have a minimum amount of ease built into the printed sloper beyond the form measurements, which allows for fitting on the dress form. The Center Front (CF) and Center Back (CB) lengths, on the bodice, are fitted to the bottom of the white waist tape positioned by the Wolf Form Co. The skirts are fitted from below this white tape. The minimum amount of circumference ease added to the slopers, beyond the dress form measurements, are:

Bust – 1"
Waist – ½"
Hip – 1"

The *dress form* takes the place of the human body. All dress form measurements are taken snugly around the dress form but must include at least the minimum amount of ease listed above. Slopers cannot be made to the exact measurements of the form. The fitting muslin would then be too tight to fit the form. Also, not all dress forms of the same size are the same, nor do they have the same amount of ease around the bust, waist, and hip. The difference in ease allowance depends upon the manufacturer.

Body measurements should be taken on a person clothed in bra, panties, and pantyhose. To establish accurate measurements, the tape measure should not be pulled too tight or too loose. The key points for measurement should be established on the body relating to the measuring points on the dress form. Follow the steps below.

1. Tie a tape measure around the waist.
2. Small tabs can be placed at:
   - Neck: CF hollow of neck; CB neck bone
   - Waistline: CF, CB, Side Seam
   - Side Seam: 2" below hollow of armhole
   - Shoulder length: below ear to shoulder bone at armhole

See illustrations in Chapter 2 for guidelines and precise positions for measuring.

The slopers should be adjusted and a full muslin should be cut and fitted. Additional ease and adjustments may be necessary before the slopers are cut in oak tag, card stock, or poster board.

Acknowledgments

I would like to express my sincere thanks and deep appreciation to the following people for their support and help in shaping and making this project possible. The Fairchild team, their professionalism, and knowledge enabled this project to move along smoothly. They were a joy to work with and I have great admiration and gratitude for all. Olga Kontzias, Executive Editor of Fairchild Books, who shared my vision for the merits of this sloper kit and instruction manual; for her advice, insight, encouragement, and sharing her knowledge. Patricia Taguer, Director of Production, for her endless hours of research, travel, and advice to finalize the Pellon® and the printer; her knowledge was invaluable. Elizabeth Marotta, Associate Production Editor, whom I worked closely with for many months. I thank her for her expertise, graciousness, and the long hours it took to put this project together. Suzette Lam, Assistant Editor; Adam B. Bohannon, Art Director, and to all who were involved with this project.

I would also like to thank the following reviewers:

Marilyn Hefferen, Drexel University; Anita Racine, Cornell University; and Susan Stark, San Francisco State University.

Very special thanks to my talented team who have been working with me on all my books—my sincere gratitude to them for their loyalty and commitment, to this project. Chao Yan Yang, who translated my hand drawn illustrations into the wonderful technical illustrations in the manual, his expertise, patience and knowledge. Hyo-Jin Choi, my former student, who worked weekends with me for many months transferring my draped muslins to oak tag, and then tracing them to paper for reproduction by the printer.

Thanks to Parsons School of Design for making my classroom available as workspace on the weekends. And finally, thanks to my husband Harry, who patiently put up with my long days and late nights of work, and for proofreading my first drafts.

Sylvia Rosen

MAKE
IT FIT

Chapter One

Tools for Slopers and Patterns

Objectives

- Identify tools for making slopers.
- Learn the purpose and use for each tool.

Professional patterns and slopers must be precisely drawn using specific tools. Shapes and lines are never drawn freehand. The tools must be used appropriately to create patterns, to blend shapes, and so as not to distort the pattern. The tools and their uses are shown in the following diagrams.

Eraser
Kneaded, soft, and medium hard

Sharpener
For mechanical lead pencil with interchangeable leads

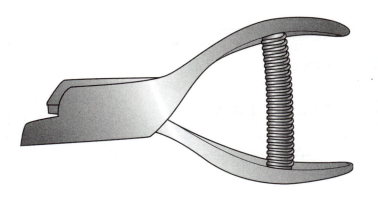

Notcher

This hand held tool used to make a ¹⁄₁₆" x ³⁄₁₆" notch on completed master patterns (slopers). Notches indicate various positions, such as pocket placement, darts, seams, and style lines. They are the key to matching pattern pieces in the sewing process.

«

Tracing Wheels

A 7" hand held tool has a wooden or plastic handle on one end and a metal wheel on the other. It is used to transfer patterns to paper or muslin, and for trueing darts and shapes. The three types of wheels used are:

Dull Point (slightly serrated) used for fabrics.

Needle Point (sharp spike points) used for paper.

Flat Wheel (no points) used for fabric and paper.

Awl

A sharply pointed small tool, with handle or all metal, is used to punch small holes at dart points, apex point, pocket placement, tucks, and various other style positions necessary for sewing information.

«

French Curve

Deeper shaped plastic *French* curves are made in various sizes and shapes and are used for blending waistlines, armholes, necklines, and style lines.

»

Sleigh Curve

A 10 ½" plastic curve is excellent for all around use in shaping waistlines, armholes, and necklines, and for blending curves and shapes.

»

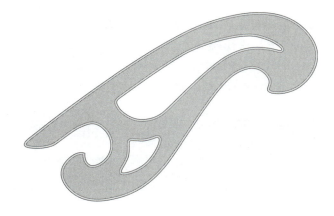

Hip Curve Stick

A 20" or 24" slightly curved metal ruler is used to shape hiplines, and hemlines, and to blend longer shapes.

«

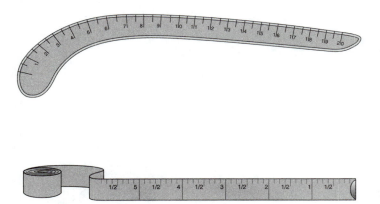

Vary Form Curve

A 24" curved ruler is for measuring curves and for creating and blending shapes.

«

Tape Measure

This is a long narrow plastic tape with inches printed on both sides, ⅝" x 60", with metal tips.

«

Small Triangle

A small plastic triangle can be used in notebooks for developing ¼" scale slopers. Used to square lines.

»

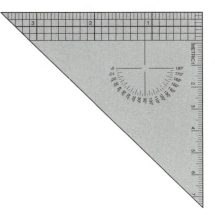

Clear Plastic Rulers (1" x 6"; 2" x 18")
Various sizes are used depending upon the areas
to be measured. Plastic transparent rulers enable
lines to be drawn precisely. »

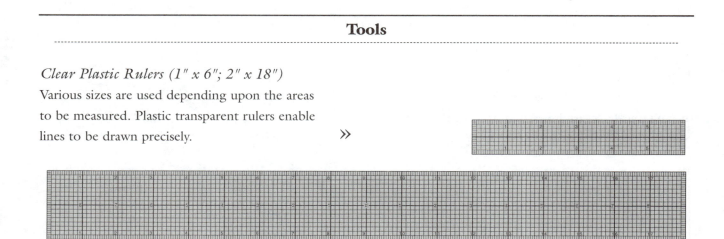

L-Square Ruler
A standard metal 14" x 24" metal L-shaped ruler is used for
drawing straight lines and to square horizontal and vertical lines
on patterns and slopers to create perfect balance.
«

Fabric Scissors
A 9" to 12" sharply pointed scissors is for
cutting fabric only. Paper and fabric scissors
should not be used interchangeably.
»

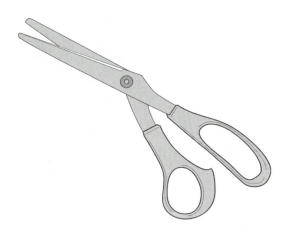

Paper Scissors
An 8 ½" to 9" scissors is for cutting paper patterns
and oak tag.
«

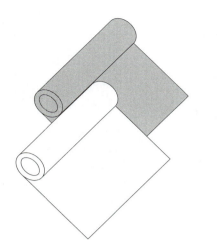

Paper

Three pattern making paper weights are used:

- White Opaque: Available in a variety of widths for plotting patterns.
- Yellow Tissue: This is available in a variety of widths for tracing off completed patterns. This paper is transparent.
- Oak Tag or Poster Board: Medium to heavy weight is available on a roll or on precut sheets. Used to trace slopers.

≪

Pencils

Various pencils are needed:

- Mechanical pencil with interchangeable size black leads is used with illustrated sharpener.
- Red and blue pencils are for corrections on paper and muslin.

≫

Pins

Silk #17 steel satin straight pins

≪

Muslin (not shown)

Use muslin for tracing completed patterns and test fitting slopers on a dress form or model, either pinned or basted. Muslin is available in several weights and should be unbleached. It can be bought by the yard or by the bolt.

- Lightweight muslin is used for draping garments on the dress form.
- Medium weight muslin is used mostly for dresses, pants, and skirts.
- Heavy weight muslin is used for outerwear garments, such as jackets and coats.

Chapter Two

Body Measurements

Objectives

- Identify major figure types.
- Learn to document accurate body measurements.
- Translate body measurements to the dress form.
- Prepare the dress form and body for measurements.

Major Figure Types

Most women fit into one of a group of figure types that are identified by the shape of their body and the relationship of the shoulder width to the bust, waist, and hips. The body types listed below are the seven major categories of figure types. Many women do not fit precisely into a specific type and may be a combination or variation of these following shapes:

- Evenly Proportioned
- Rectangle
- Pear
- Apple
- Hourglass
- Diamond
- Round

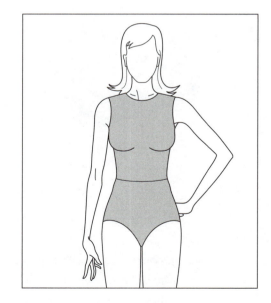

Evenly Proportioned

Bust is either slightly smaller than hip, or the same width as hip, with a smaller waist.

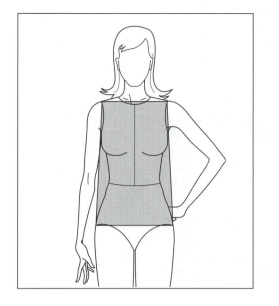

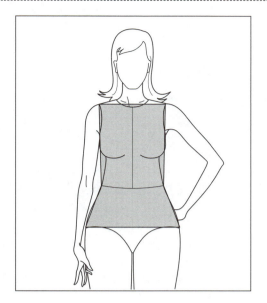

Rectangle

A thinner straight body that gives a tubular look, due to narrow shoulders and hips. The wider waist has a square look.

Pear

The shoulders, bust, and waist are narrow in comparison to wider, fuller hips and thighs.

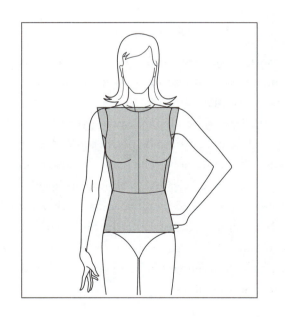

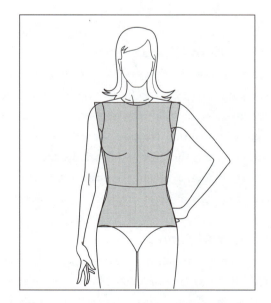

Apple

This body type is the opposite of the pear shape, with wider, larger shoulders, upper arms and abdomen that taper to narrow, flat hips and thighs. This type usually has thin legs.

Hourglass

This body has a very small waist in relationship to full bust and hips that are usually of the same curvaceous proportions.

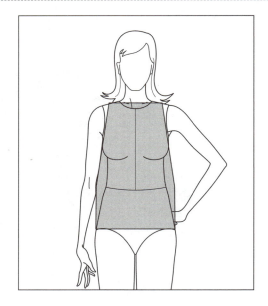

Diamond

This body type usually has narrow shoulders and hips and thinner legs. The waist and abdomen are very wide and rounded by comparison, giving the body a diamond shape.

Round

This body type has full and rounded upper arms and thighs, with a wide full abdomen, giving the body a rounded or circular shape.

Analyze Your Figure

Now that you've identified the major figure types, analyze your own figure to determine which category you fit into. In the following sections, you will learn the steps of measuring the body or a dress form—an important part in the process of making patterns that fit all body shapes. You will also learn the relationship between the body and the dress form measurements.

Measure and Chart

Step one is to accurately measure and precisely document all the body measurements, both vertical and horizontal, on the charts. These charts are the road map for adapting and adjusting slopers, master patterns, or commercial patterns to fit. See the following page for an example of a worksheet for recording measurements.

The charts for documenting measurements have several columns that need to be filled in. The pat-

terns will be adjusted to fit based on these measurements. It is important to measure carefully from point to point for maximum accuracy.

The body should be measured over a body suit or underwear, and tabs can be positioned at the key points of measurement. The points of measurement on the dress form are clearly established by tapes and seam lines positioned by the manufacturer. We need to establish these same points on the body. The following illustrations show vertical and horizontal measurements for the front and back bodice, sleeve, and crotch measurements.

Add Minimum Wearing Ease

After the measurements are documented following the charts, minimum wearing ease is added to the horizontal measurements. This is very important to add, as this is the basic ease that is built into the garment for movement or for sitting. Without this ease, the fitting garment would be too tight for the body and dress form. After the basic ease is totaled into the measure- ments, and the patterns are fitted and perfected, design ease is added to the patterns based on fabric, style, and desired fit. This will be charted later in the manual.

Form or Body Measurements—Do not Include Ease

	6	8	10	12	14
BODICE					
CFL–center front length					
CBL–center back length					
FULL front length—from high shoulder pt.					
FULL back length—from high shoulder pt.					
SHOULDER SLOPE					
front					
back					
WAIST–full circumference					
front					
back					
SHOULDER–neck to shoulder bone					
NECK CIRCUMFERENCE					
front					
back					
SIDE SEAM–½" below armplate to bottom of form waist tape					
WIDTH ACROSS SHOULDERS					
front					
back					
BUST—full body width–2" below armplate					
front					
back					
BODY WIDTH–½" below armplate					
DIAPHRAGM–under bust					
DIAPHRAGM-midway between bust & waist					
BUST–around neck for halter					
BREAST POINT–from shoulder neck to apex point					
ACROSS BUST–APEX TO APEX POINT—plus or minus ⅛"					
WIDTH ACROSS CHEST–3" below neck, armhole to armhole					
WIDTH ACROSS BACK-4" below neck, armhole to armhole					
ARMHOLE–from shoulder ridge (bone) around to ½" below armplate					
ARMHOLE DEPTH–from shoulder. Ridge over armplate, to 2" below armplate					
CENTER FRONT–waist to princess line					
CENTER BACK–waist to princess line					
BNS–back neck to shoulder seam + or - ⅛"					
CERVICAL HEIGHT–stature					

Worksheet for Recording Measurements

Form or Body Measurements—Do not Include Ease

	6	8	10	12	14
HEAD height					
HEAD CIRCUMFERENCE					
WAIST to FLOOR					
TORSO–for skirts and pants					
CFL–center front length to hem or ankle					
CBL–center back length to hem or ankle					
WAIST circumference					
front					
back					
HIGH HIP circumference–3"–4" below waist					
front					
back					
HIP circumference–7 ½"–8 ½" below waist					
front					
back					
CROTCH circumference W. to W.–center front waist					
through crotch to center back waist					
CROTCH DEPTH–at side seam sitting measure waist to chair					
THIGH–upper circumference at crotch					
THIGH–middle					
KNEE circumference–with knee bent					
KNEE height–to waist					
CALF circumference					
ANKLE circumference					
SLEEVE					
OVERARM LENGTH–with arm bent—					
from shoulder ridge (bone) to wrist bone					
UNDERARM LENGTH–1" below armpit					
BICEPS circumference–around fullest part of upper arm					
ELBOW circumference–with arm bent					
WRIST–loosely around wrist					
CAP HEIGHT–from biceps to shoulder ridge (bone)					
FULL SLEEVE LENGTH–from center back neck bone straight					
down to wrist bone (with arm slightly bent)					

Vertical Measurements for Front Bodice

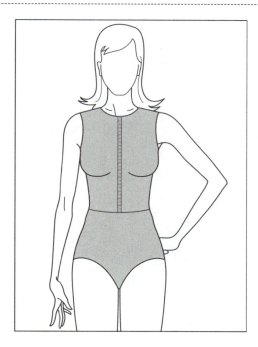

Center Front Length

Measure from hollow of neck to waist, loosely over bust area.

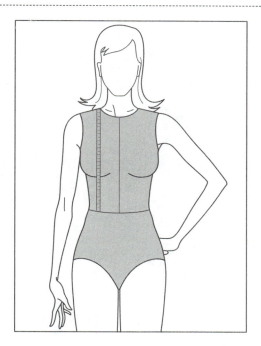

Full Front Length

Measure from high shoulder neck point to waistline.

Front Shoulder Slope

Measure from bone at shoulder diagonally to center front waistline.

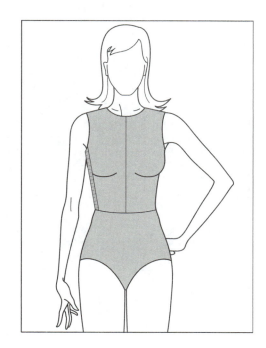

Side Seam

Measure 2" below hollow of armpit to waistline.

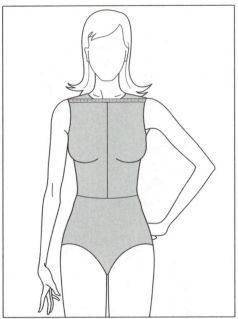

Width Across Shoulders

Measure straight across from shoulder bone to shoulder bone.

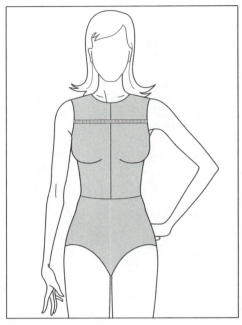

Across Chest

Measure 3" below hollow of neck, then measure from armhole to armhole.

Body Width

Measure 1" below hollow of armpit; or ½" below armplate on form.

Front Bust

Measure from side seam to side seam across fullest part of bust, about 2" below top of side seam measurement.

Horizontal Measurements for Front Bodice

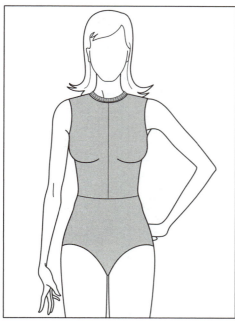

Front Neck

Measure from high shoulder neck point around front of neck.

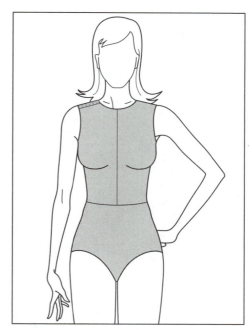

Shoulder Length

Measure from shoulder point of neck to shoulder bone.

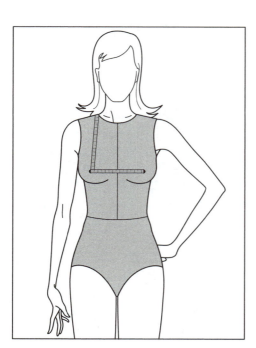

Breast Point Position

Measure from shoulder point to apex, across bust, from apex point to apex point.

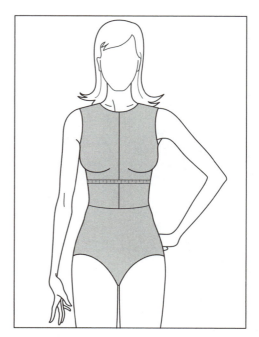

Midriff

Measure from side seam to side seam, 4 ½" up from waist.

Horizontal Measurements for Front Bodice

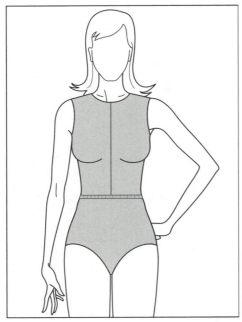

Front Waist

Measure from side seam to side seam.

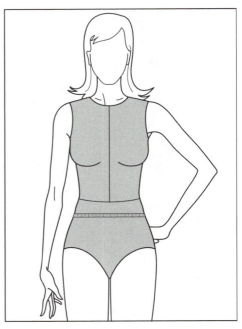

High Hip

Measure 3" to 4" below waistline, from side seam to side seam.

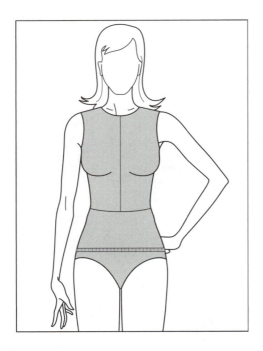

Full Front Hip

Measure 7" to 8" below waistline, from side seam to side seam.

Full Low Hip

Measure across fullest part of hip, at upper thigh, approximately 9" to 10" below waistline.

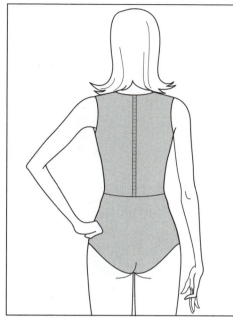

Center Back Length
Measure from nape of neck to waist.

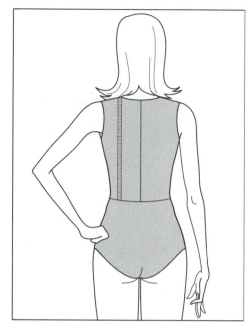

Full Back Length
Measure from high shoulder neck point to waistline.

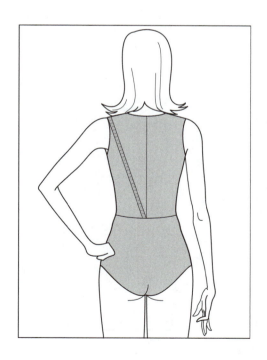

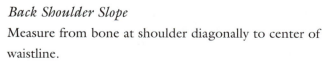

Back Shoulder Slope
Measure from bone at shoulder diagonally to center of waistline.

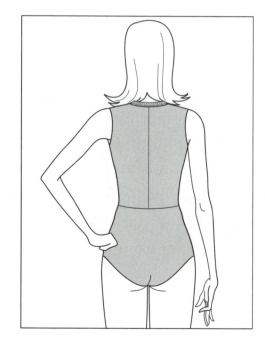

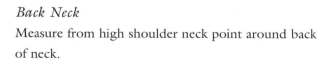

Back Neck
Measure from high shoulder neck point around back of neck.

Horizontal Measurements for Back Bodice

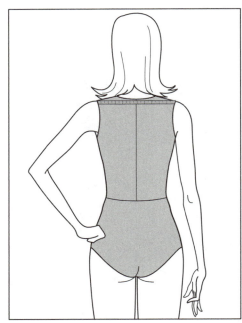

Width Across Shoulders

Measure straight across, from shoulder bone to shoulder bone.

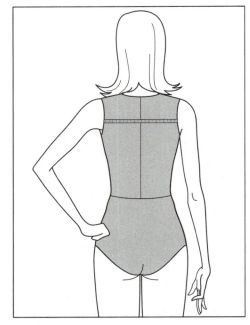

Across Back

Measure 4" below nape of neck, from armhole to armhole.

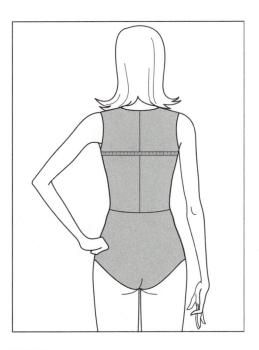

Body Width

Measure straight across, 1" below hollow of armpit, or ½" below armplate on dress form.

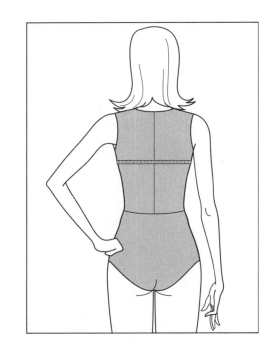

Full Back Width (Bust Level)

Measure from side seam to side seam across fullest part of the back; about 2" below top of side seam measurement.

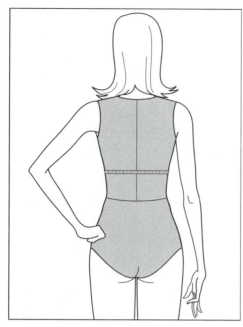

Midriff

Measure 4 ½" up from waistline, from side seam to side seam.

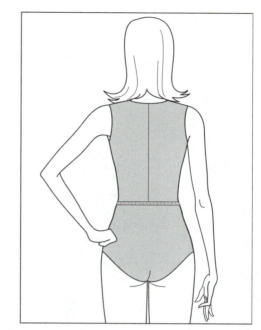

Back Waist

Measure from side seam to side seam.

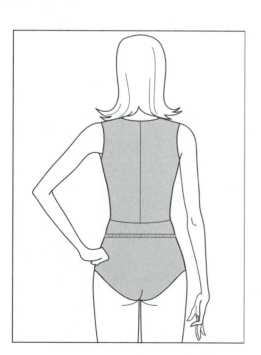

High Hip

Measure 3" to 4" below waistline, from side seam to side seam.

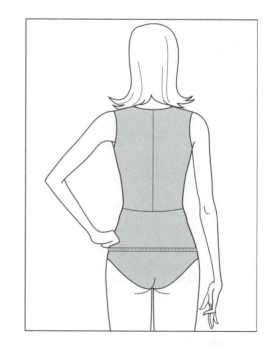

Full Back Hip

Measure about 7" to 8" below waistline, from side seam to side seam.

Horizontal Measurements for Back Bodice

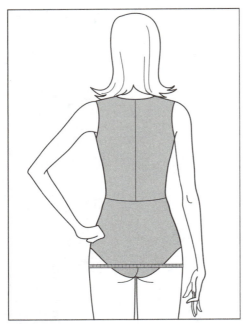

Full Low Hip

Measure across fullest part of hip, approximately 9" to 10" below waistline.

Horizontal and Vertical Sleeve Measurements

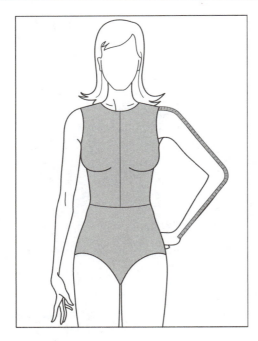

Sleeve Length

Measure, with arm bent, from bone at shoulder to bottom of wrist bone.

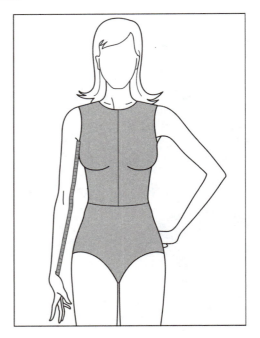

Underarm Length

Measure from 2" below hollow of armpit to bottom of wristbone.

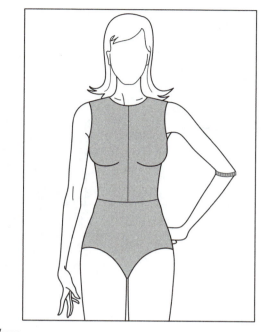

Elbow

Measure, with arm bent, around full elbow.

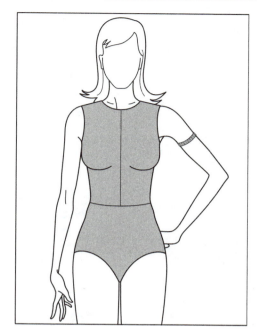

Biceps (Upper Arm)

Measure muscle, at fullest part of arm, about 2" below hollow of armpit.

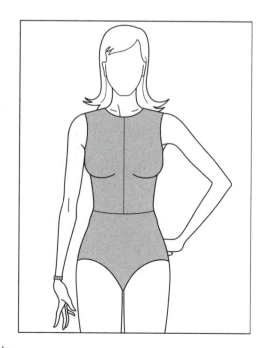

Wrist

Measure loosely arount wrist bone.

Crotch Depth – Sitting

Sit on chair, tie tape measure around waist. Measure from waist to chair.

Crotch Depth – Standing

Tie tape measure around waist. Use L-square ruler to measure depth from waist through crotch.

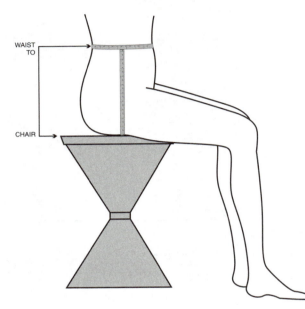

Full Crotch Length

Measure circumference from front waist through crotch to back waist.

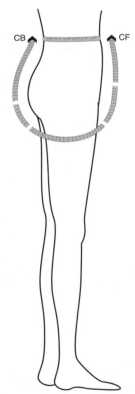

Inseam

Standing, measure from crotch to ankle.

Pants – Crotch Measurements

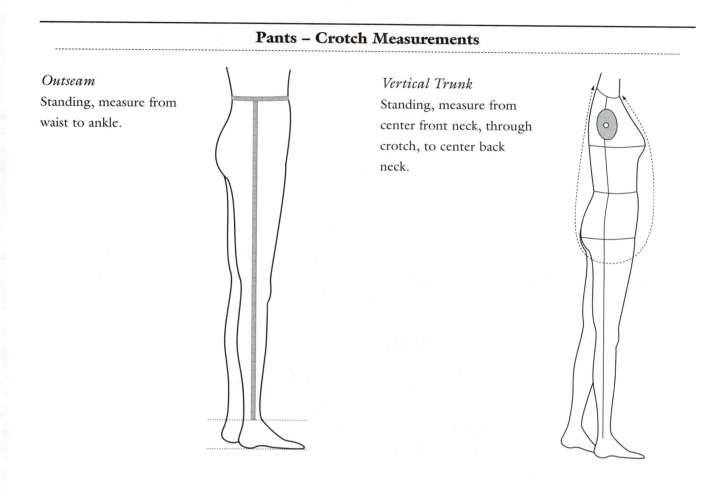

Outseam

Standing, measure from waist to ankle.

Vertical Trunk

Standing, measure from center front neck, through crotch, to center back neck.

The Body's Front Vertical Points of Measurement

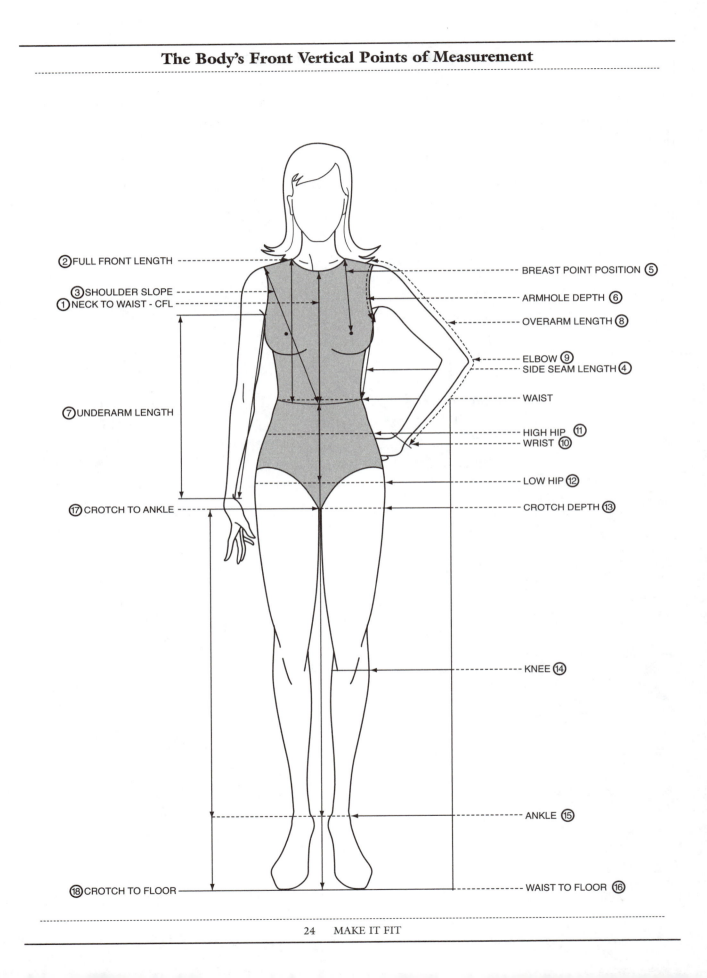

② FULL FRONT LENGTH

③ SHOULDER SLOPE
① NECK TO WAIST - CFL

⑦ UNDERARM LENGTH

⑰ CROTCH TO ANKLE

⑱ CROTCH TO FLOOR

BREAST POINT POSITION ⑤

ARMHOLE DEPTH ⑥

OVERARM LENGTH ⑧

ELBOW ⑨
SIDE SEAM LENGTH ④

WAIST

HIGH HIP ⑪
WRIST ⑩

LOW HIP ⑫

CROTCH DEPTH ⑬

KNEE ⑭

ANKLE ⑮

WAIST TO FLOOR ⑯

The Body's Front Vertical Points of Measurement

	Body or Form	Pattern Measurement	Minimum Measurement	+ or - Ease Added	Total
BODY–BODICE			0		
1. Neck to waist–CFL			0		
2. Full front length			0		
3. Shoulder slope			0		
4. Side seam length			0		
5. Breast point position			0		
6. Armhole depth			0		
SLEEVE					
7. Underarm length			0		
8. Overarm length			0		
9. Elbow			0		
10. Wrist			0		
LENGTH					
11. Waist to high hip			0		
12. Waist to low hip			0		
13. Waist to crotch			0		
14. Waist to knee			0		
15. Waist to ankle			0		
16. Waist to floor			0		
17. Crotch to ankle			0		
18. Crotch to floor			0		

The Body's Front Horizontal Points of Measurement

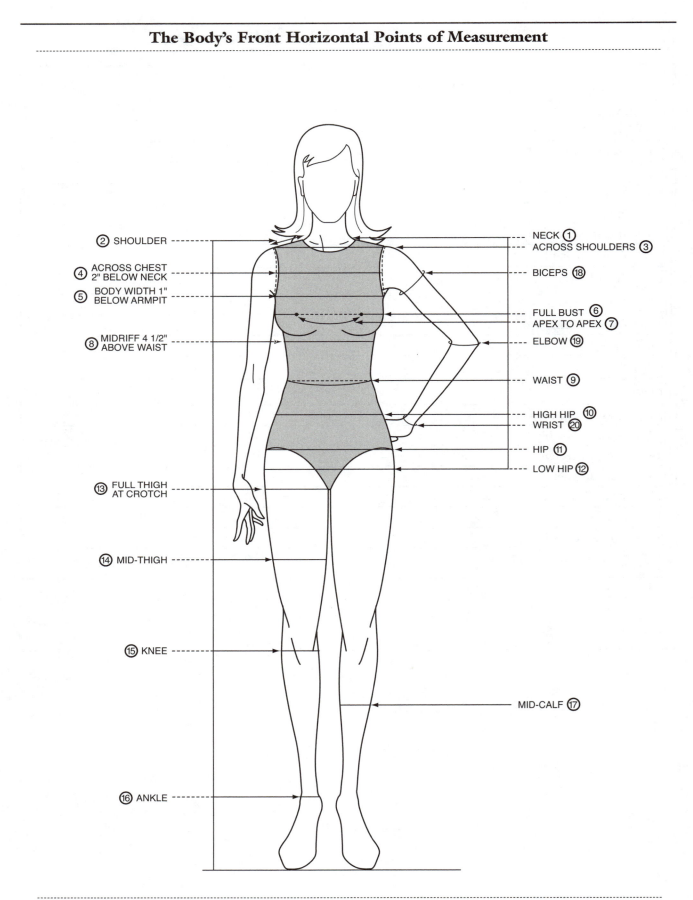

② SHOULDER

④ ACROSS CHEST
2" BELOW NECK

⑤ BODY WIDTH 1"
BELOW ARMPIT

⑧ MIDRIFF 4 1/2"
ABOVE WAIST

⑬ FULL THIGH
AT CROTCH

⑭ MID-THIGH

⑮ KNEE

⑯ ANKLE

NECK ①
ACROSS SHOULDERS ③

BICEPS ⑱

FULL BUST ⑥
APEX TO APEX ⑦
ELBOW ⑲

WAIST ⑨

HIGH HIP ⑩
WRIST ⑳

HIP ⑪

LOW HIP ⑫

MID-CALF ⑰

The Body's Front Horizontal Points of Measurement

		Body or Form Measurement	Pattern Measurement	Minimum Ease Added	+ or -	Total
BODY–BODICE						
1.	Neck			⅛"		
2.	Shoulder length			⅛"		
3.	Across shoulders			⅛"		
4.	Across chest at 2" below neck			¼"		
5.	Body width 1" below armpit			½"		
6.	Full bust			1"		
7.	Apex to apex			0		
8.	Midriff 4 ½" above waist			½"		
HIP						
9.	Waist			½"		
10.	High hip–3" to 4" below waist			¾"		
11.	Hip–7" to 7 ½" below waist			1"		
FULL CIRCUMFERENCE						
12.	Low hip–9" to 10" below waist			1"–1 ½"		
13.	Full thigh—at crotch			2"–3"		
14.	Mid-thigh			1"–2"		
15.	Knee			1"–2"		
16.	Ankle			1"–2"		
17.	Mid-calf			1"–2"		
ARM						
18.	Biceps			2"		
19.	Elbow—bent			1 ½"		
20.	Wrist			¾"–1"		

The Body's Back Horizontal and Vertical Points of Measurement

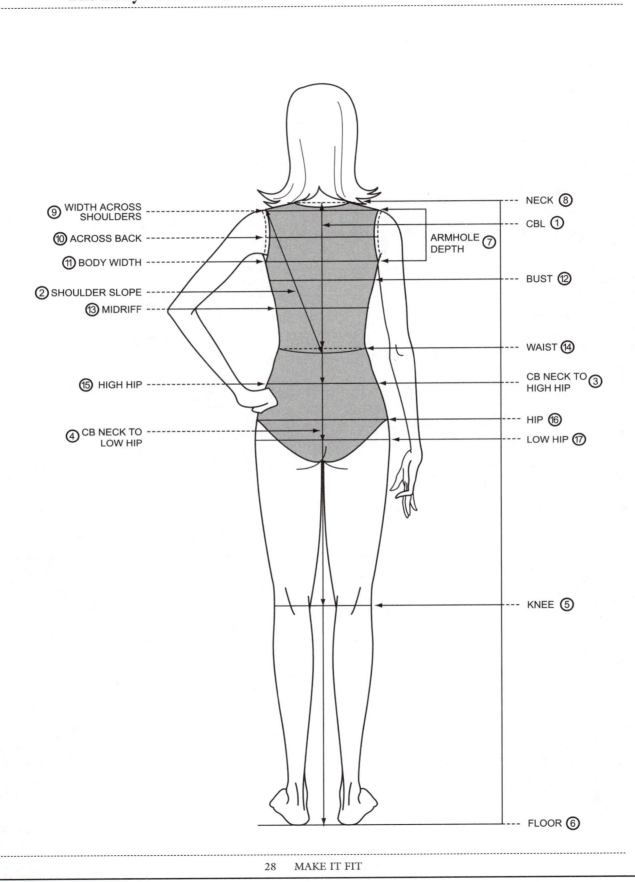

⑨ WIDTH ACROSS SHOULDERS

⑩ ACROSS BACK

⑪ BODY WIDTH

② SHOULDER SLOPE

⑬ MIDRIFF

⑮ HIGH HIP

④ CB NECK TO LOW HIP

NECK ⑧

CBL ①

ARMHOLE DEPTH ⑦

BUST ⑫

WAIST ⑭

CB NECK TO HIGH HIP ③

HIP ⑯

LOW HIP ⑰

KNEE ⑤

FLOOR ⑥

The Body's Back Horizontal and Vertical Points of Measurement

		Body or Form Measurements	Pattern Measurements	Minimum Ease Added	+ or -	Total
VERTICAL:						
BODY						
1.	Center back length–neck to waist			0		
2.	Shoulder slope			0		
3.	Center back neck to high hip			0		
4.	Center back neck to low hip			0		
5.	Center back neck to knee			0		
6.	Center back neck to floor			0		
7.	Armhole depth			0		
HORIZONTAL:						
BODICE						
8.	Neck			⅛"		
9.	Across shoulders			⅛"		
10.	Across back–4" below neck			¼"		
11.	Body width			½"		
12.	Back bust level			1"		
13.	Midriff			½"–¾"		
HIP						
14.	Waist			½"		
15.	High hip at 3"–4" below waist			¾"		
16.	Hip at 7"–7 ½" below waist			1"		
17.	Low hip at 9"–10" below waist			1"–1 ½"		

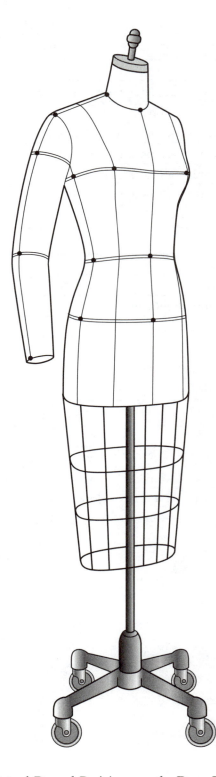

The figure to the right shows the horizontal positions to be taped that are necessary for precise points of measurement on the body. It also shows the dotted positions established on the form that correspond to exact positions on a person. These dotted points are necessary to precisely fit a garment.

To prepare the dress form, you must first establish the horizontal positions with ¼" black style tape. Then pin tape to form with pins 1" apart to keep tapes from slipping. Use the following guidelines:

Bust: Set tape 2" below armplate, parallel to floor. Pin from apex to apex around dress form, keeping the tape taut. The tape should be pinned firmly from apex to apex, but kept loose between the apex points.

Waist: The waistline is taped by the manufacturer. This tape is not parallel to the floor. The missy and women's body shape dips lower in the back than in the front.

Hip: This tape is positioned parallel to the floor. It is positioned 7 ½" to 8" below the waist, measuring from the center front waistline. The waist to hip at center front is approximately ½" to ⅝" longer than the waist to hip at center back.

Taped and Dotted Positions on the Dress Form

The Dress Form

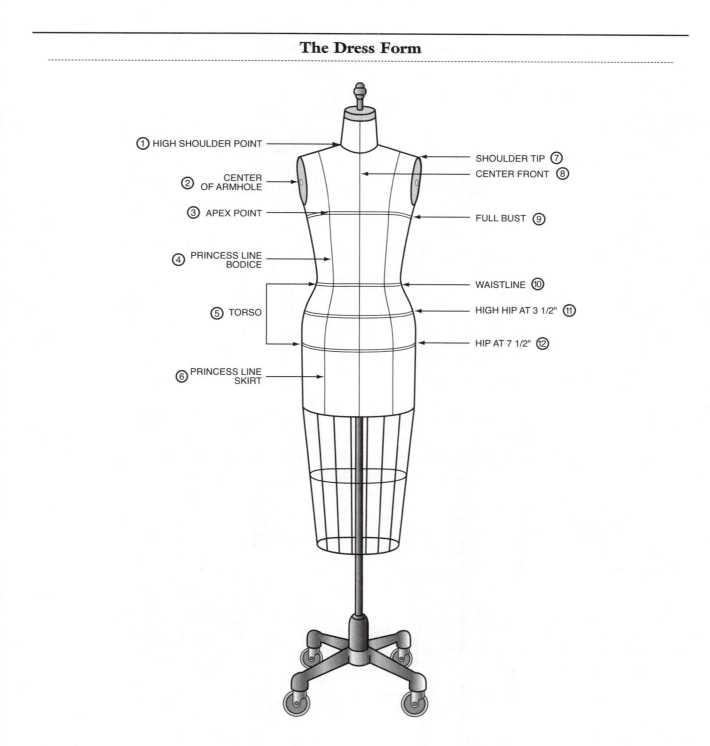

① HIGH SHOULDER POINT

② CENTER OF ARMHOLE

③ APEX POINT

④ PRINCESS LINE BODICE

⑤ TORSO

⑥ PRINCESS LINE SKIRT

SHOULDER TIP ⑦

CENTER FRONT ⑧

FULL BUST ⑨

WAISTLINE ⑩

HIGH HIP AT 3 1/2" ⑪

HIP AT 7 1/2" ⑫

Front Reference Points of the Dress Form

1. High shoulder point
2. Center of armhole
3. Apex point
4. Princess line, bodice
5. Torso
6. Princess line, skirt

7. Shoulder tip
8. Center front
9. Full bust
10. Waistline
11. High hip at 3 ½"
12. Hip at 7 ½"

Sportswear and Pant Form

Front and Back Torso Positions on Forms

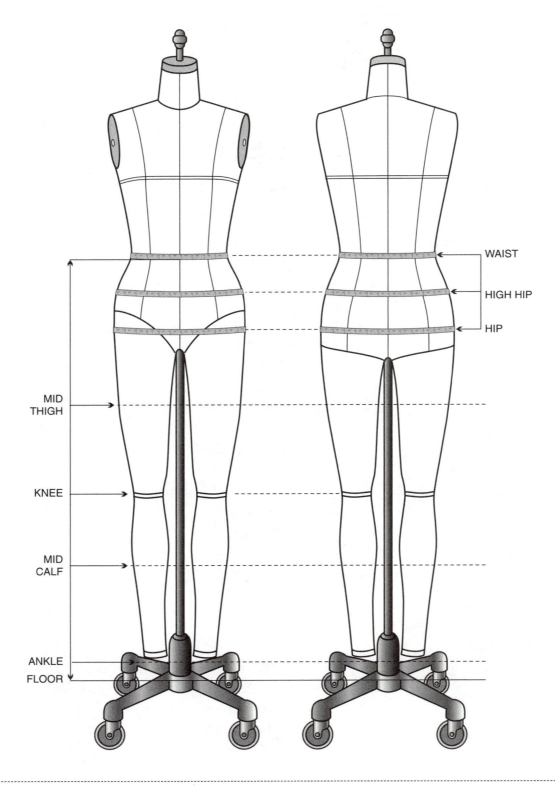

WAIST

HIGH HIP

HIP

MID THIGH

KNEE

MID CALF

ANKLE

FLOOR

Pant Lengths

Pant Lengths as They Relate to Points on the Form

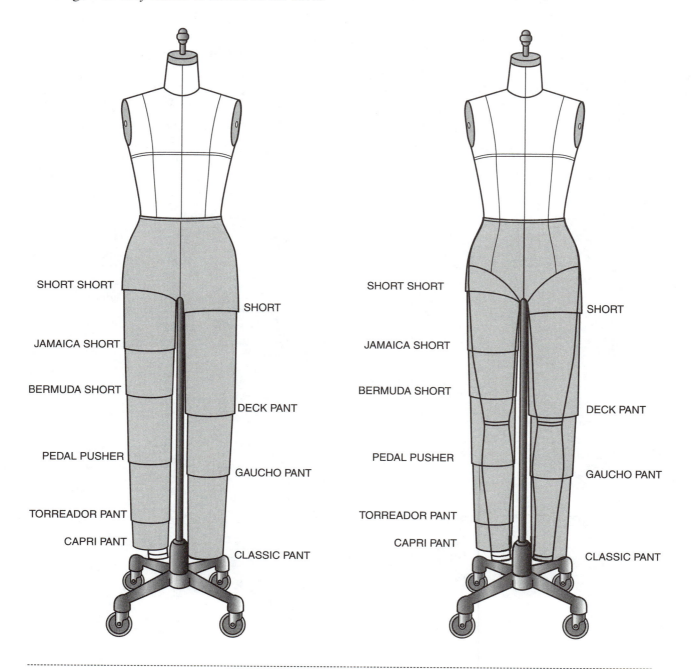

SHORT SHORT

SHORT

JAMAICA SHORT

BERMUDA SHORT

DECK PANT

PEDAL PUSHER

GAUCHO PANT

TORREADOR PANT

CLASSIC PANT

CAPRI PANT

Skirt Lengths as They Relate to Points on the Form

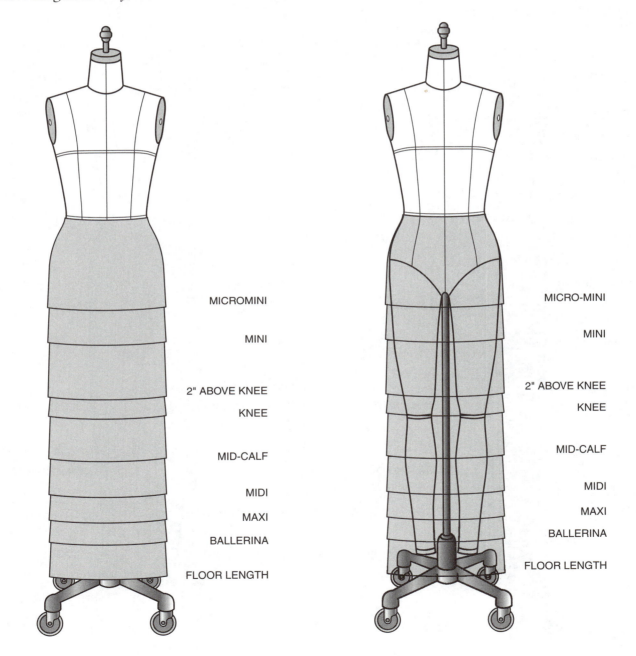

MICROMINI

MINI

2" ABOVE KNEE

KNEE

MID-CALF

MIDI

MAXI

BALLERINA

FLOOR LENGTH

MICRO-MINI

MINI

2" ABOVE KNEE

KNEE

MID-CALF

MIDI

MAXI

BALLERINA

FLOOR LENGTH

Chapter Three

Using the Sloper Kit

Objectives:

- Become familiar with the slopers and sub-slopers in the kit.
- Recognize slopers illustrated on a body.
- Learn about additional sub-slopers that can be developed from the slopers in the kit.

Slopers and Sub-slopers

The slopers enclosed in the *Make It Fit* kit, numbered 1–15, are the basis for making all slopers and patterns. The basic slopers are:

- 2-dart straight skirt (#2)
- Basic bodices (#5)
- 1-dart long sleeve (#10)
- Long straight sleeve (#11)
- Basic 2-dart pant (#15)

The remaining slopers in the kit (numbered 1, 3, 4, 6, 7, 8, 8a, 9, 12, 13, and 14) are all sub-slopers. They are constructed from the basic slopers listed above. For example, the bodice numbers 7, 9, and 12 all have larger armholes and are used with the sleeve slopers 8 and 8a. The following section summarizes the slopers in the *Make It Fit* kit.

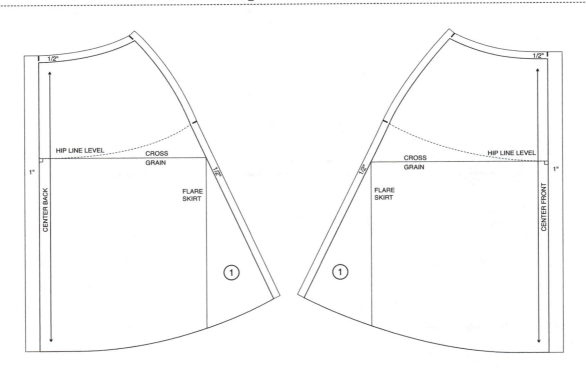

Sloper 1 Flared Skirt
Front and Back

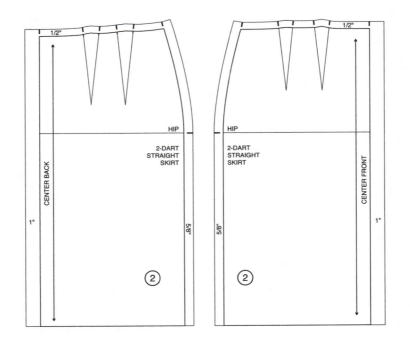

Sloper 2 2-Dart Straight Skirt
Front and Back

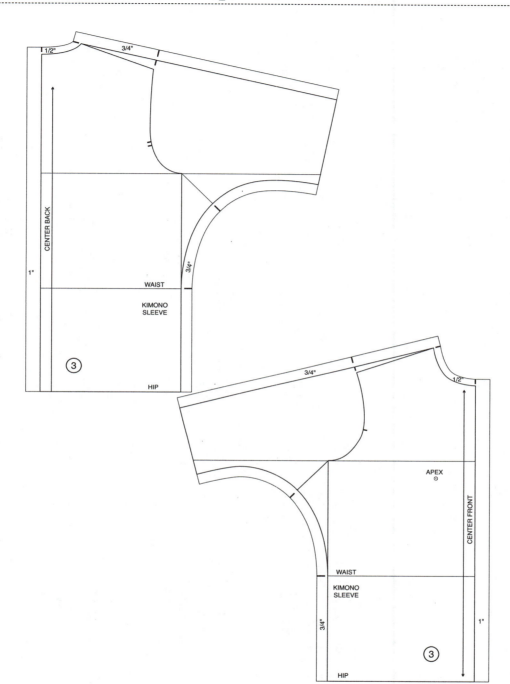

Sloper 3 Kimono Sleeve Torso
Front and Back–elbow sleeve length

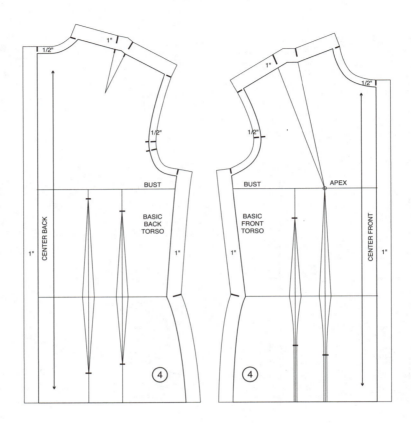

Sloper 4 Torso

Front – 2 waist darts – 1 shoulder dart

Back – 2 waist darts – 1 shoulder dart

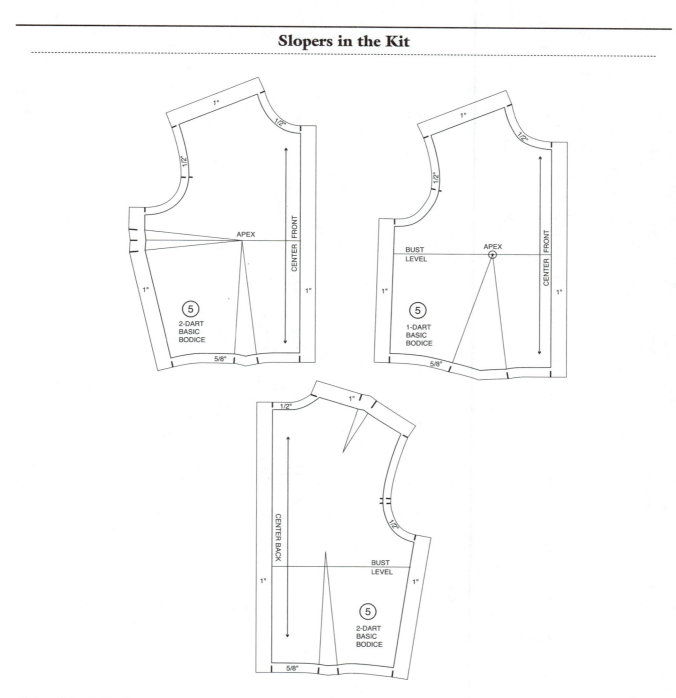

Sloper 5 Basic Bodices

Front – waist dart

Front – bust and waist dart

Back – shoulder and waist dart

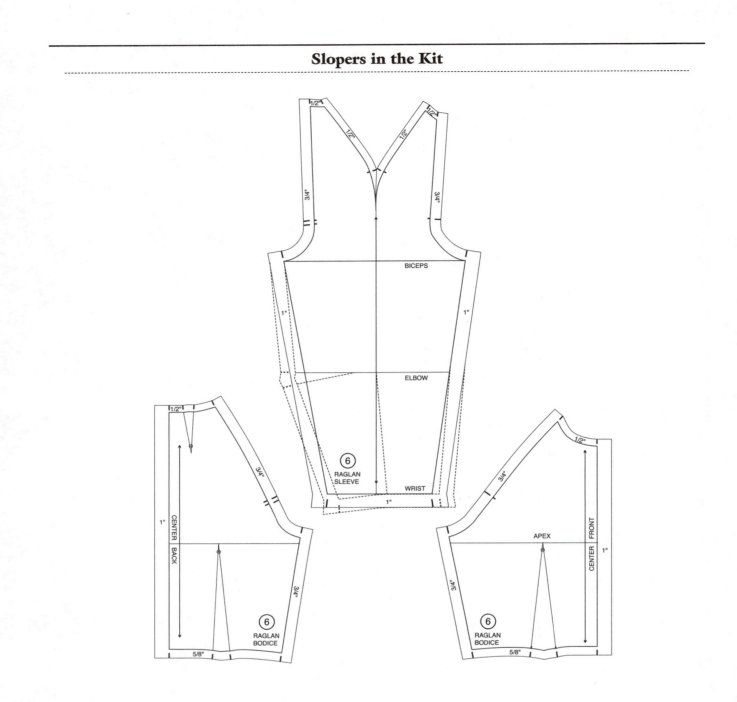

Sloper 6 Raglan Bodice

Front – waist dart

Back – waist and shoulder darts

Raglan Sleeve–shoulder dart

Long sleeve – 1-dart shaped

Long sleeve – straight

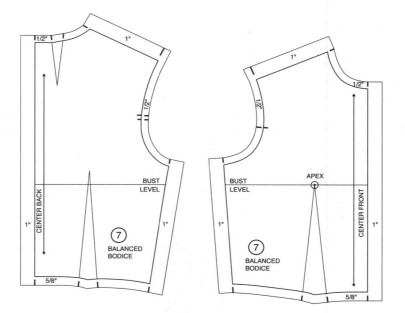

Sloper 7 Balanced Bodice

Front – waist dart

Back – waist and neck dart

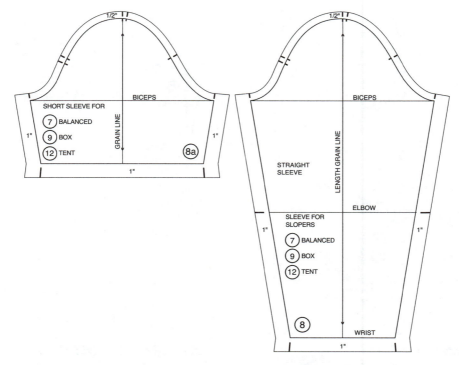

Sloper 8a Balanced Short Sleeve

Front and Back Balanced Slopers (7)

Front and Back Tent Slopers (12)

Sloper 8 Balanced Long Sleeve

For: Front and Back Box Slopers (9)

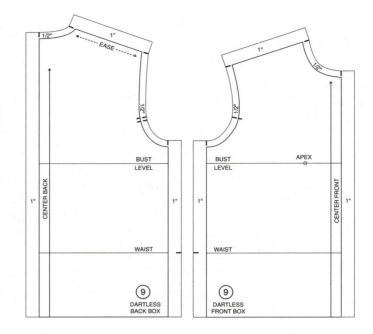

Sloper 9 Box Torso Sloper

Front and Back Torso Straight Shift

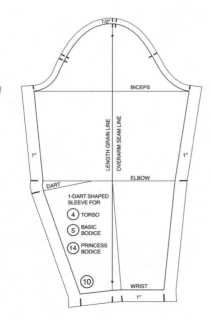

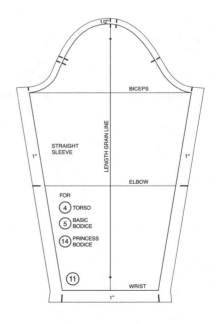

Sloper 10 One-Dart Long Sleeve

For: Basic Bodice (5)

      Princess Bodice (14)

      Torso Sloper (4)

Sloper 11 Long Straight Sleeve

For: Basic Bodice (5)

      Princess Bodice (14)

      Torso Sloper (4)

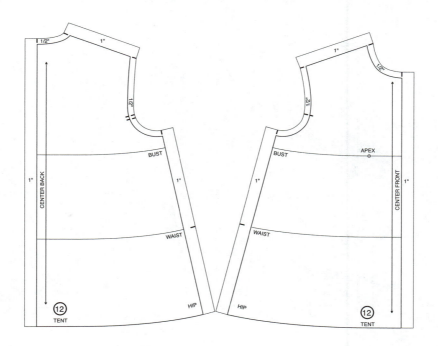

Sloper 12 Tent Torso Sloper
Front and Back A-Line

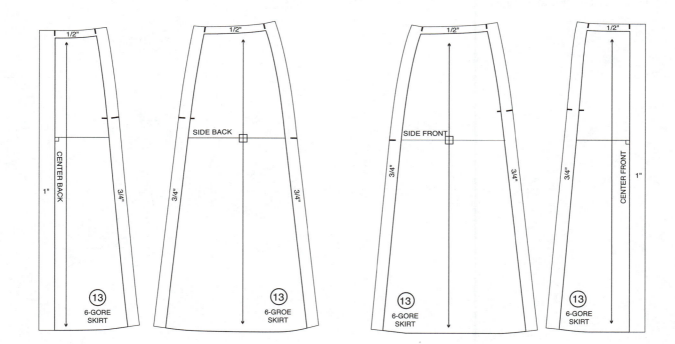

Sloper 13 Six-Gore Skirt
Front and Back A-Line

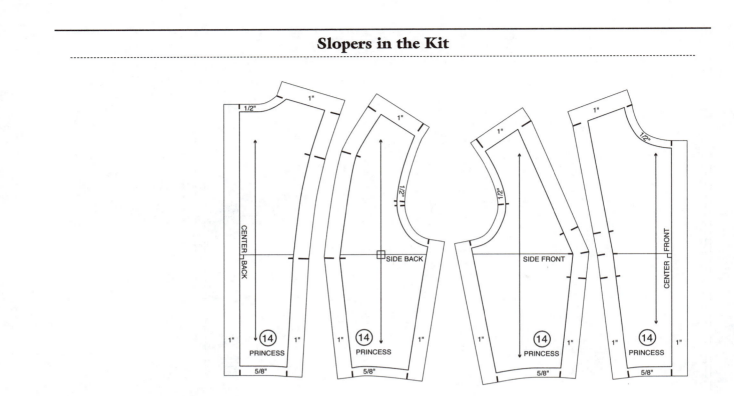

Sloper 14 Princess Bodice
Front and Back Shoulder Princess

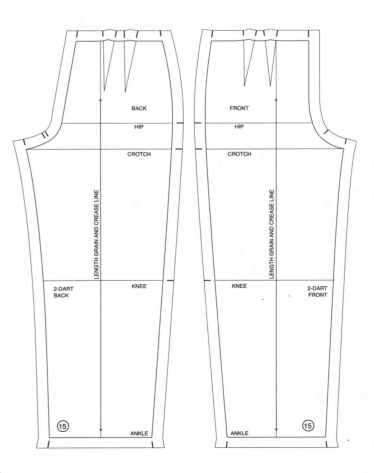

Sloper 15 Basic 2-Dart Pant
Front – 2 waist darts
Back – 2 waist darts

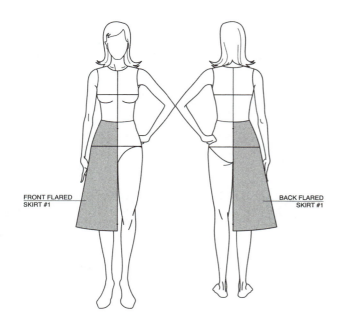

FRONT FLARED
SKIRT #1

BACK FLARED
SKIRT #1

The following illustrations show how each sloper fits the body.

Flared Skirt #1
Front and back flare
≪

Straight Skirt #2
Front skirt, 2 darts
Back skirt, 2 darts
≫

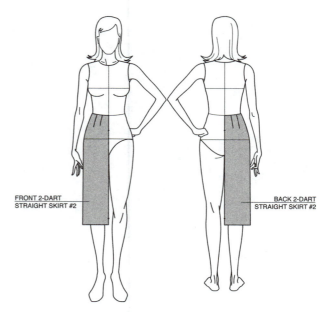

FRONT 2-DART
STRAIGHT SKIRT #2

BACK 2-DART
STRAIGHT SKIRT #2

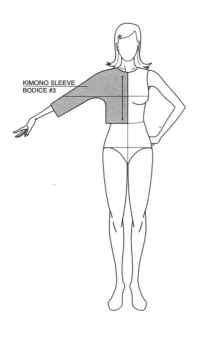

KIMONO SLEEVE
BODICE #3

Kimono Sleeve Bodice #3
Front—sleeve to elbow. Please note that the back kimono is the same as the front with a higher neck.
≪

Torso Sloper #4

Front–2 waist darts, 1 bust dart

Back–2 waist darts, 1 shoulder dart

Sleeve #10, elbow dart; can also use sleeve #8

»

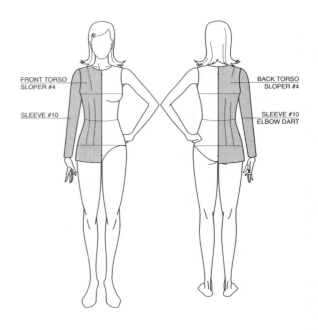

FRONT TORSO
SLOPER #4

BACK TORSO
SLOPER #4

SLEEVE #10

SLEEVE #10
ELBOW DART

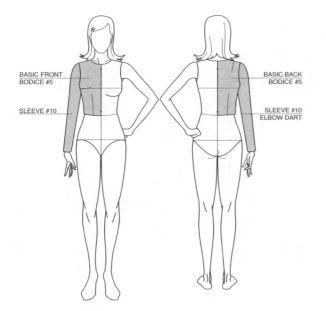

BASIC FRONT
BODICE #5

BASIC BACK
BODICE #5

SLEEVE #10

SLEEVE #10
ELBOW DART

Basic Bodice #5

Front–bust and waist dart

Back–shoulder and waist dart

Sleeve #10–elbow dart

«

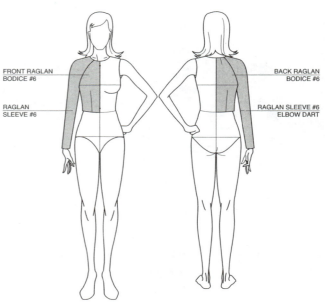

FRONT RAGLAN
BODICE #6

BACK RAGLAN
BODICE #6

RAGLAN
SLEEVE #6

RAGLAN SLEEVE #6
ELBOW DART

Raglan Bodice #6

Front and back–waist dart

and shoulder dart

Sleeve #6–elbow dart

»

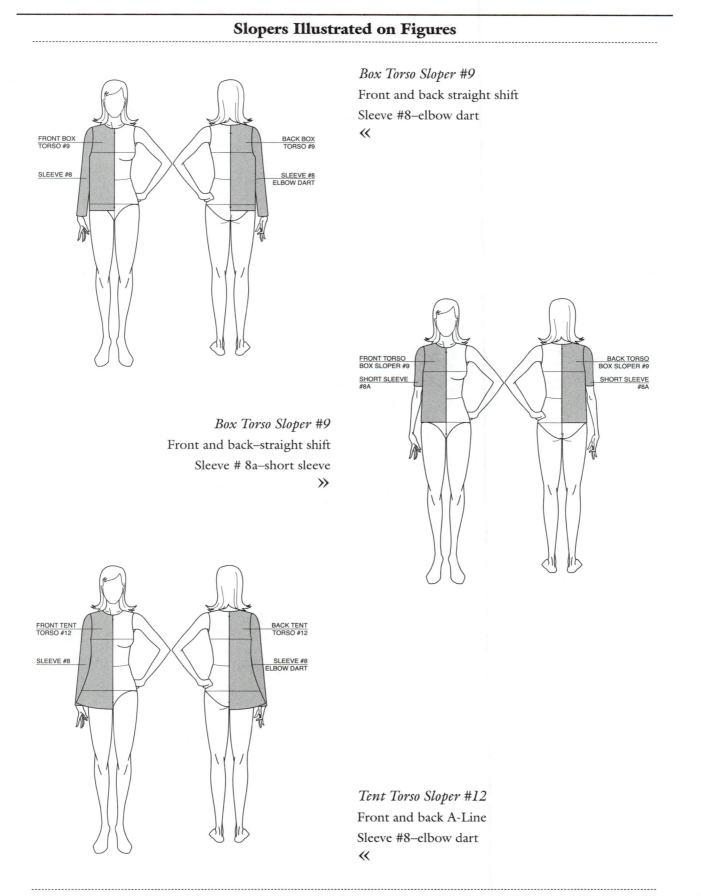

Box Torso Sloper #9
Front and back straight shift
Sleeve #8–elbow dart
«

FRONT BOX
TORSO #9

BACK BOX
TORSO #9

SLEEVE #8

SLEEVE #8
ELBOW DART

Box Torso Sloper #9
Front and back–straight shift
Sleeve # 8a–short sleeve
»

FRONT TORSO
BOX SLOPER #9

BACK TORSO
BOX SLOPER #9

SHORT SLEEVE
#8A

SHORT SLEEVE
#8A

FRONT TENT
TORSO #12

BACK TENT
TORSO #12

SLEEVE #8

SLEEVE #8
ELBOW DART

Tent Torso Sloper #12
Front and back A-Line
Sleeve #8–elbow dart
«

Slopers Illustrated on Figures

Six Gore Skirt #13

Front and back gore seams

»

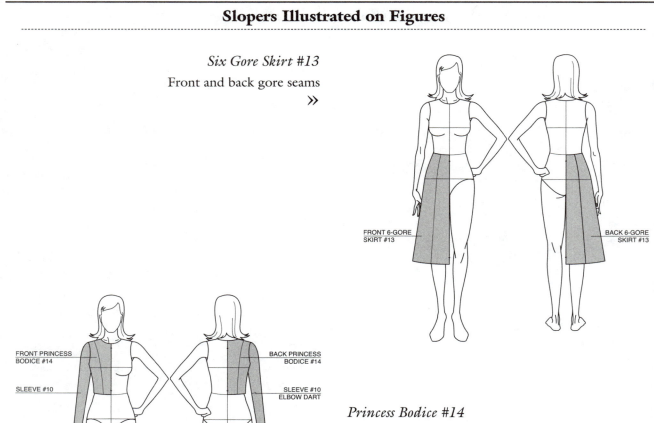

FRONT 6-GORE
SKIRT #13

BACK 6-GORE
SKIRT #13

FRONT PRINCESS
BODICE #14

BACK PRINCESS
BODICE #14

SLEEVE #10

SLEEVE #10
ELBOW DART

Princess Bodice #14

Front and back princess seams

Sleeve #10, elbow dart;

    can also use sleeve #8

«

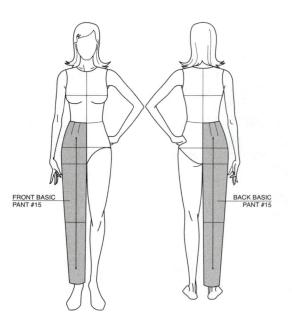

FRONT BASIC
PANT #15

BACK BASIC
PANT #15

Basic Pant #15

Front—2 waist darts

Back—2 waist darts

»

All slopers and sub-slopers can go through an additional process of development to create many more sub-slopers and variations of the basics.

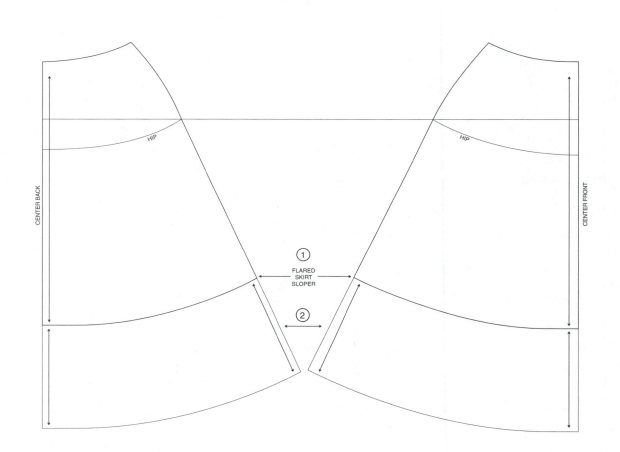

Front and Back Flared Skirt to Longer Skirt
(sloper 1)

- The flared skirt shown is lengthened proportionally by measuring and equally extending the center front and the side seam to calf or ankle length skirt.

- This adjusted sloper could be added to the *Make It Fit* kit.

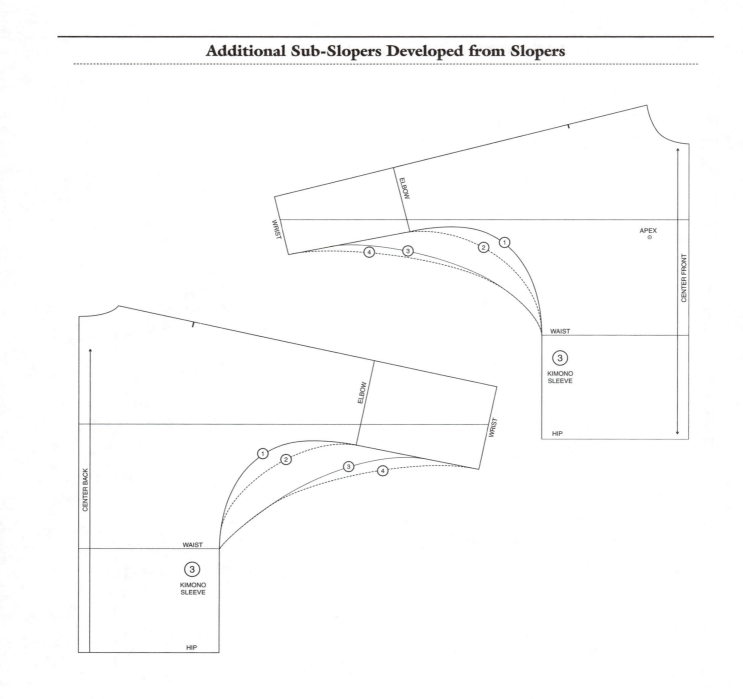

Front and Back Kimono Sleeve Sloper to Kimono/Dolman Sleeve Variations (sloper 3)

- The Basic ¾" length kimono sleeve can be reshaped at the underarm.
- (1) is the original basic shape in the *Make It Fit* kit.
- (2) shows a deeper kimono shape.

- (3) and (4) show the conversion to a dolman sleeve from waist to wrist.
- There are many more variations that can be made from this Sloper depending upon the style and the amount of underarm fullness desired.
- Any one of these variations can be added to the *Make It Fit* kit.

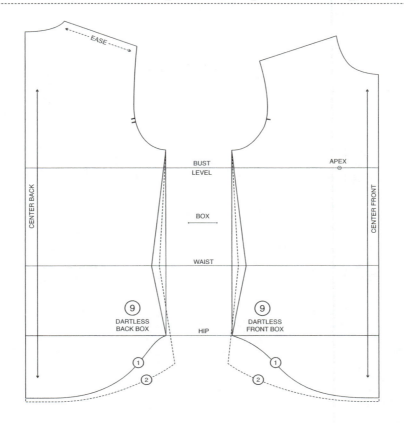

Dartless Front and Back Box Sloper to Shirt Slopers (sloper 9)

- The box sloper can easily be converted to the basic shirt sloper with variations of hem shapes and waist fullness or closer fit. The lines are all interchangeable depending on what final shape is desired. The box can be shaped at the waist and the hem shape can vary.

- (1) The solid line is shown as a shirt sloper shaped in 1" at the waistline and with a shaped hem.

- (2) The dotted line is shown as a wider, longer shirt sloper, shaped in ½" at the waist and with a longer wider hem shape.

- These new shirt shapes could also be added to the *Make It Fit* kit.

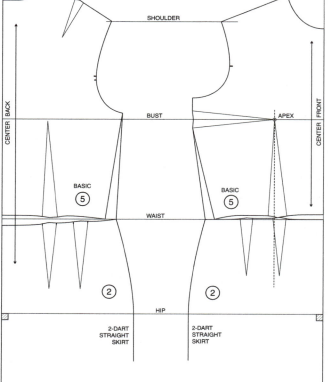

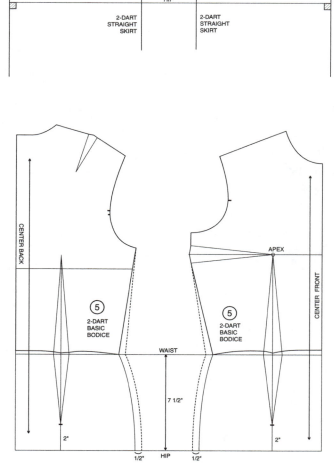

Additional Sub-Slopers Developed from Slopers

Front and Back Bodice Sloper to One-Dart Torso Sloper (sloper 5)

The two-dart basic bodice sloper can be converted to a basic torso bodice sloper with one front and back waist dart using bodice slopers #5.

To convert:

- Follow illustration. Draw a vertical line for the center front. Square a horizontal line from the center front representing the waistline.
- Draw another vertical line parallel to the center front allowing space for the center back bodice.
- Place center front and center back bodice touching both vertical lines, and waistline resting on the horizontal line.

«

- Extend center front and center back 7 ½" to 8" for hip length. Square across and connect from center front to center back.
- Connect hip to waist with curve.
- Lengthen bodice dart to 2" above hip. Connect at waist to form one long dart.
- On a torso sloper, the center of the dart, from apex point to 2" above hip should be parallel to the center front and center back. The dart may need to be repositioned for this.
- Use dotted lines for additional ease.
- Trace and cut out in oak tag and add to *Make It Fit* kit.

Chapter Four

Adjusting Slopers for Fit

Objectives:

- Learn the rules for balance and fit.
- Learn to adjust bodices, sleeves, skirts, and pants.

Balance and Fit

The patterns enclosed in this kit can be adjusted to fit a form or body. By following the diagrams in this chapter, you will learn how to properly adjust the slopers. When fitting slopers on a dress form, the printed Pellon® patterns can be cut out, and the ½ patterns can be pinned together. They can also be traced to oak tag and then cut out to keep the original printed patterns intact. See chapter 5 for detailed instructions on tracing, cutting, and testing slopers.

The following list explains ten important rules for achieving balance and fit:

1. The lines that should be perpendicular to the floor are:
   - Side seam, center front, and center back seams.
   - Length grains, front and back.
   - Length grain on sleeve.

2. Bodice darts:
   - Point to fullest part of the bust, the apex.
3. Shoulder seams:
   - Should end at shoulder bone.
   - Should be in center of shoulder, not pulling to the front or back.
4. Garment front and back:
   - Should have ease but not wrinkle.
   - Should not pull horizontally or vertically.
5. Neckline:
   - Should not ride up.
   - Should sit flatly around the neck.
6. Sleeves:
   - Need ease so as not to twist or pull to the front or back.
   - Should not have wrinkles in cap, but ease in smoothly to armhole.
   - Length grain should be perpendicular to the floor and line up with the side seam.

7. Waistline:
   - Should not pull up, wrinkle, or be too tight.
   - Should fit smoothly and easily around body.

8. Hips, front and back:
   - Garment should sit on the body with ease so as not to wrinkle or pull.
   - If garment is too tight, darts can be adjusted and more ease added to side seams.

9. Zippers:
   - Should meet at center front or center back without pulling open, or more ease would need to be added.

10. Pant Crotch:
    - Front should fit without wrinkles or smile lines.

- Back should not hang loose or baggy.
- Should not be too tight and pull in to the body.

Adjusting Slopers

NOTE: The measurements shown on diagrams for increasing, decreasing, raising, lowering, and adjusting are examples showing how and where to adjust slopers. The actual adjustments and measurements should be based on ease needed after fitting.

All sleeves must also be adjusted to fit the corresponding changes on the bodices. The following diagrams show basic bodice alterations for fit.

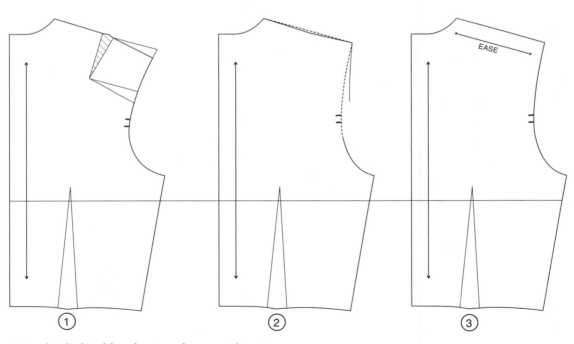

Eliminating back shoulder dart and converting to ease

1. Slash or pivot dart into armhole.
2. Blend shoulder.
3. Ease shoulder.

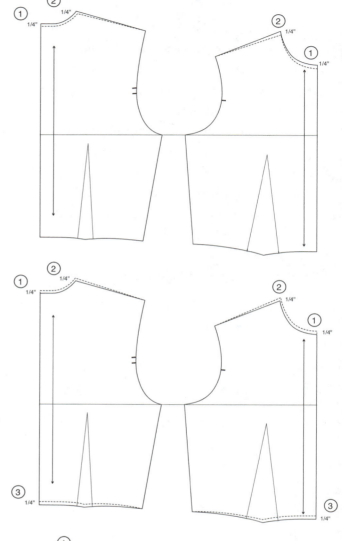

For square shoulders

1. Lower neckline at CF and CB ¼" or desired amount.
2. Lower shoulder ¼" at neck to 0" at shoulder / armhole.

For sloping shoulders

1. Raise CF and CB neckline ¼".
2. Raise shoulder ¼" at neck to 0" at shoulder.
3. Raise CF and CB waistline ¼" to 0" at side seams.

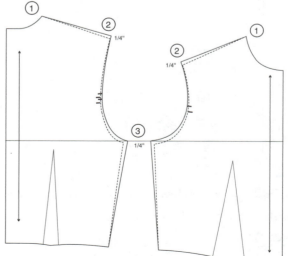

For low shoulders

1. Adjust 0" at neck.
2. Lower ¼" at shoulder.
3. From 0" at upper armhole, lower armhole ¼" at side seam to 0" at waist.

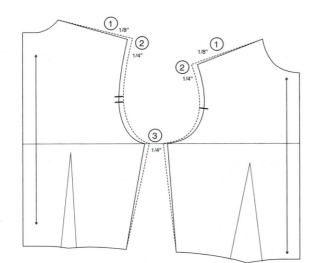

For additional ease

1. Raise shoulder ⅛" at shoulders.
2. Extend shoulder and armhole out ¼".
3. Extend armhole out ¼" down to 0" at waist.

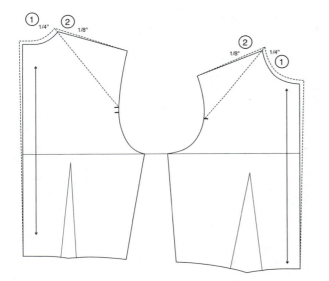

For fuller front and back and longer neck

1. Raise neckline ¼" at CF and CB neck to shoulder.
2. Raise shoulder ⅛" at neck to 0" at shoulder.

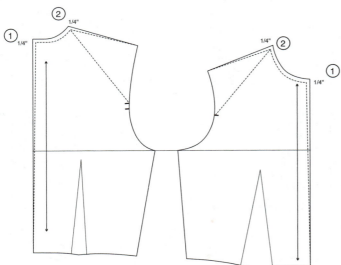

For a short neck

1. Lower CF and CB ¼" at neck to 0" at waist
2. Lower shoulders ¼" at neck to 0" at shoulder / armhole.

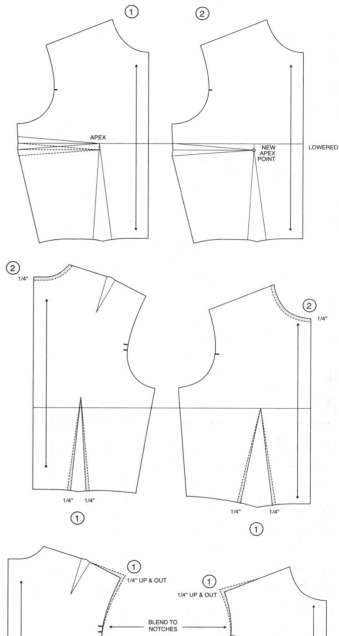

To lower bust dart

1. Lower bust dart to desired position depending on fit.

2. Lower apex point to meet the lowered bust dart and position new apex.

For wider waist darts and lower neckline

1. Measure ¼" or desired amount on each side of dartlegs, decrease and redraw to 0" at point of darts.

2. Lower neckline ¼" or desired amount evenly to shoulder.

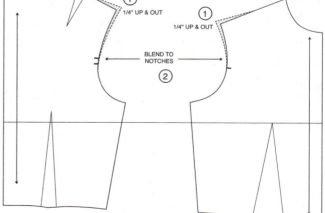

For wider and higher shoulders

1. Raise shoulder ¼" from middle of shoulder to armhole.

2. Extend shoulder out ¼" and blend down to notches on armhole.

Adjust Your Bodices

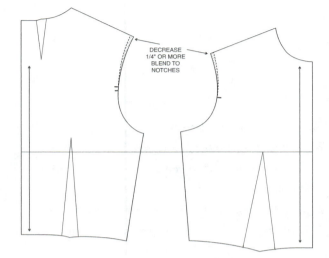

For narrow shoulders

1. Decrease shoulder length ¼" or more and blend to notches.

Complex Bodice Adjustments

NOTE: The measurements shown on the diagrams are examples showing how to adjust slopers. The actual adjustments should be based on the actual ease needed after fitting.

When adjusting slopers to add on or decrease shoulders, armholes, and side seams, sleeves must also be adjusted to fit.

For longer neck, higher shoulder, and to add fullness at side seam, front and back bodice are both adjusted.

1. Raise shoulder ¼".
2. Square out ¾" (or desired amount) at armhole / side seam down to.
3. ¼" at waist.
4. Lower neckline at center front ½" to 0" at shoulder.
5. Lengthen shoulder seam ⅛" at armhole.

Sleeve cap would be adjusted, and ¾" would be added to side seams.

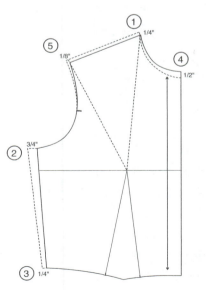

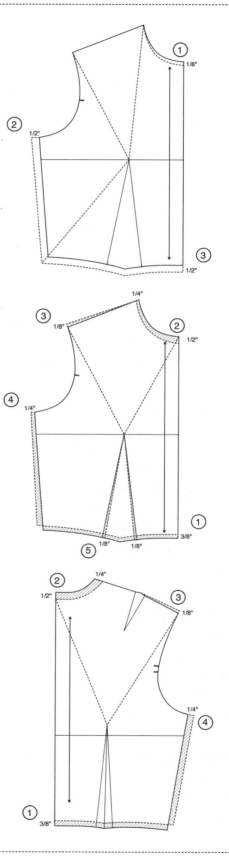

For lower neckline, longer bodice, and wider side seam, front and back bodice are both adjusted.

1. Lower neckline ⅛" at center front to 0" at neck / shoulder.

2. Square out ½" at armhole down to waistline.

3. Lengthen ½" from center front waist to side seam.

Front and Back Bodice

For shorter bodice, longer neck, square shoulders, wider armhole and side seam, and smaller dart, front and back bodice are both adjusted.

1. Shorten waist ⅜".

2. Lower neckline ½" at CF to ¼" at neck / shoulder.

3. Raise shoulder at armhole ⅛" to 0" at neck.

4. Square out at armhole and widen side seam ¼" down to waist.

5. Decrease front dart ⅛" on each dartleg.

Back Bodice

Follows steps 1–4 above. Waist dart can be smaller or remain as is.

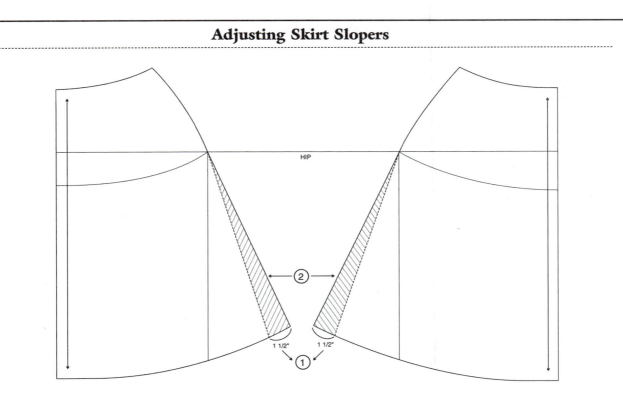

To Decrease Flared Skirt

1. Measure desired amount at hem on side seam and blend to 0" at hip.

2. To keep skirt balanced, the same amount must be increased or decreased on front and back hemline.

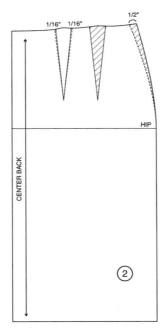 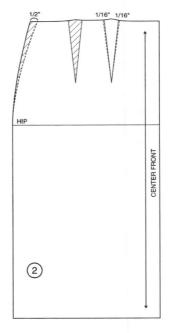

Skirt converted to 1-dart from a 2-dart sloper

1. Measure dart and remove at side seam blending into hip curve. Retrue waistline by folding dart and blending with hip curve.

2. Blend off any points for a smooth fit.

3. Add or subtract within the seam allowance for additional ease or tighter fit. Redraw new seam allowance.

Sleeve bodice adjustments

NOTE: The measurements shown on the diagrams are examples showing how to adjust sleeves and slopers. Sleeves must be adjusted depending on the changes made on side seams, armholes, and shoulders.

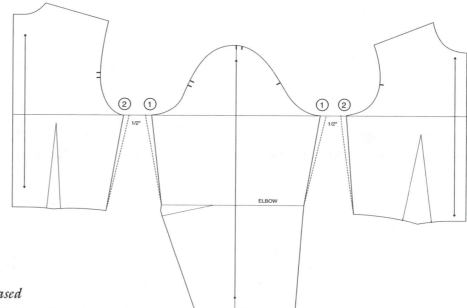

Biceps and armhole increased

1. Increase biceps ½" on each side of the sleeve to 0" at elbow.
2. Increase side seam at armhole ½" down to 0" at waist.

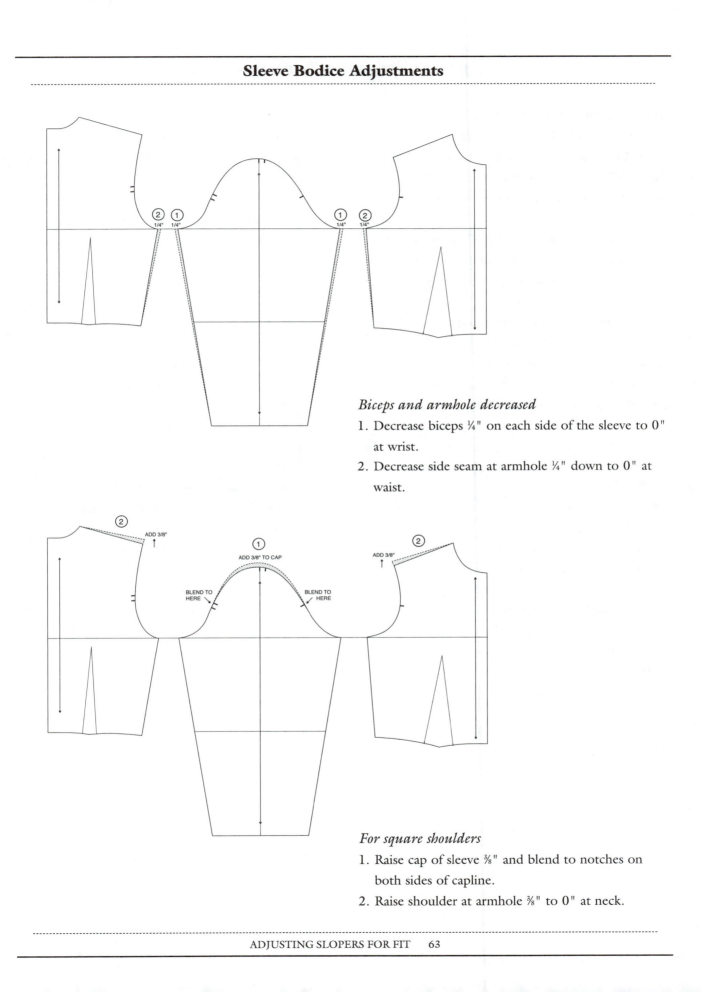

Biceps and armhole decreased

1. Decrease biceps ¼" on each side of the sleeve to 0" at wrist.
2. Decrease side seam at armhole ¼" down to 0" at waist.

For square shoulders

1. Raise cap of sleeve ⅜" and blend to notches on both sides of capline.
2. Raise shoulder at armhole ⅜" to 0" at neck.

Walking the Sleeve Around the Armhole

After the sloper bodices are adjusted in the shoulder, armhole, and side seams for more or less ease, the sleeve will need to be adjusted to fit any changes. The format for doing this is shown in the diagrams and is referred to as "walking the sleeve."

The sleeve should be "walked" around the armhole to determine the amount of ease in the cap. The notches on the cap will also need to be repositioned if any changes have been made.

The amount of ease in the cap varies, usually from ¾" to 1 ¼" for a basic sleeve. The ease is distributed equally between the front, back, and shoulder cap notches. Sleeve caps have notches positioned according to the following process:

- Determine the cap height by measuring from the biceps to the top of the cap. This is called cap height.
- The sleeve will have a length grain that divides the biceps width in half.
- Measure and divide the cap height in half.
- As shown on all the sleeve slopers, two notches are positioned at the back half and one notch is positioned at the front half.
- A length grain notch is positioned at the top of the cap to indicate grain line.

- A shoulder notch is positioned ¼" to the front of the length grain. This shoulder notch, when the sleeve is sewn into an armhole, lines up with the shoulder seam. This pulls the sleeve slightly forward, following the natural forward bend of the arm in its natural position.

The notches are always positioned on the cap and then pivoted into the armhole as diagrammed on the next page. The steps for pivoting are:

1. Begin by positioning the bicep corner of the sleeve to the side seam corner of the bodice armhole.
2. Using a pushpin on cork or cardboard, walk the sleeve cap around the armhole up to the sleeve cap notch. Mark notch on armhole at this point.
3. Continue walking the sleeve until the sleeve cap touches the shoulder point of the bodice. Crossmark cap at this point.
4. This crossmark determines the amount of ease on each side of the shoulder notch. If more or less ease is needed in the cap, it can be adjusted at this time for a smooth fitting set-in cap.

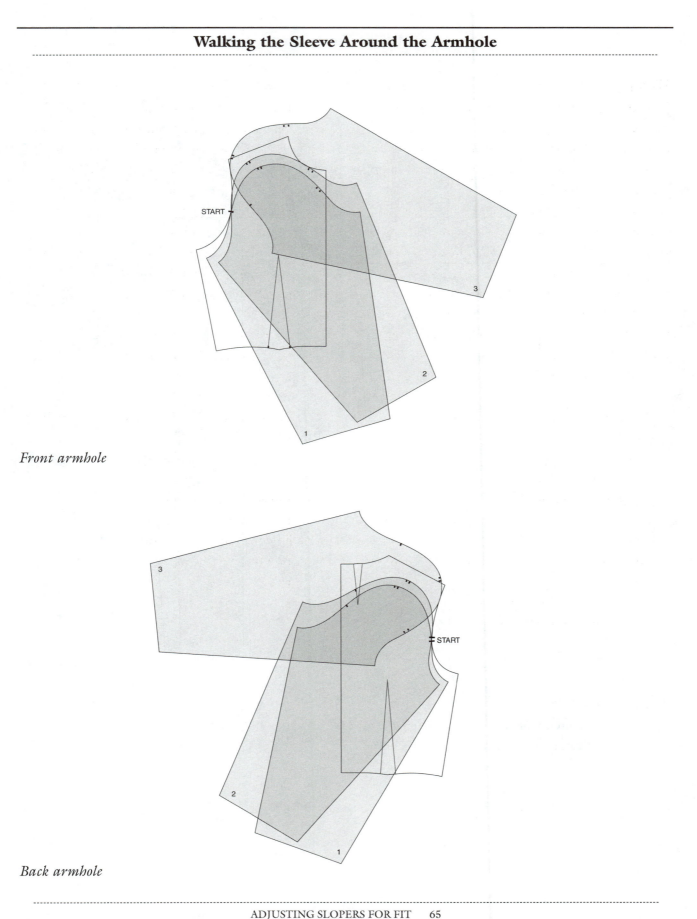

Front armhole

Back armhole

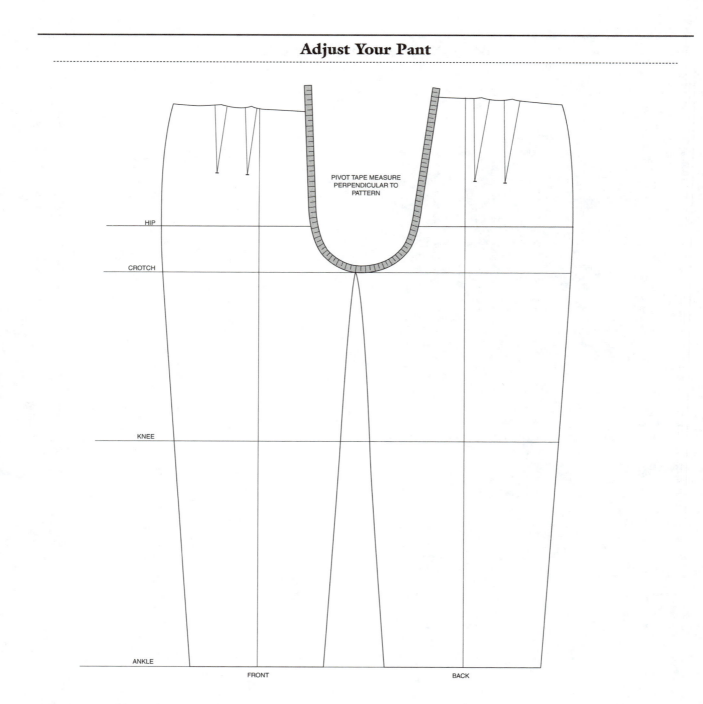

PIVOT TAPE MEASURE
PERPENDICULAR TO
PATTERN

HIP

CROTCH

KNEE

ANKLE

FRONT

BACK

Measure crotch

1. Use tape measure to measure full crotch length.

2. Pivot tape measure perpendicular to pattern.

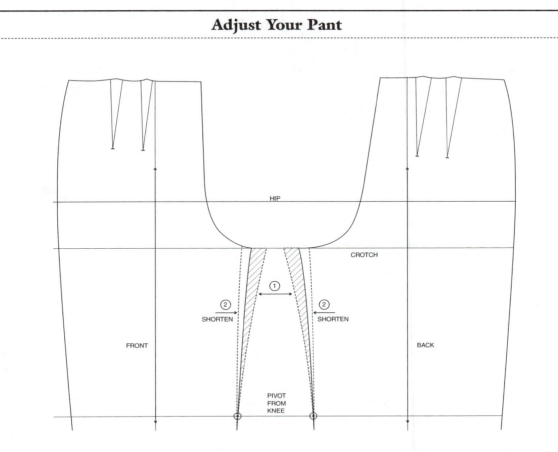

To lengthen or shorten crotch

1. To lengthen crotch and add fullness to upper thigh, pivot from knee and blend desired amount to crotch.

2. To shorten crotch and decrease fullness to upper thigh, pivot from knee and blend to crotch.

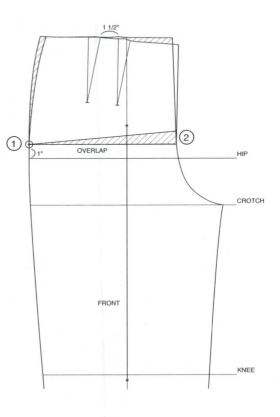

To shorten crotch—front and back

1. To shorten front or back crotch, overlap desired amount from front or back to side seam above hip.

2. Blend crotch line.

»

To lengthen crotch–front and back

1. Slash front crotch to above hip.
2. Pivot from side seam and spread desired amount.
3. Blend crotch line.

»

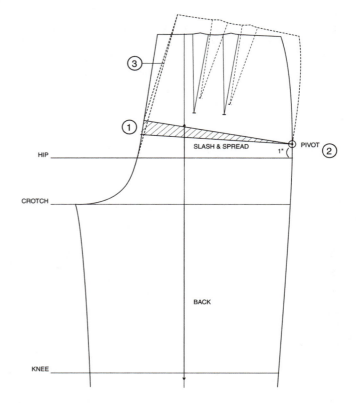

To loosen a tight crotch–front and back

1. Lengthen crotch curve ¼" or to desired amount.
2. Blend to 0" at waist.

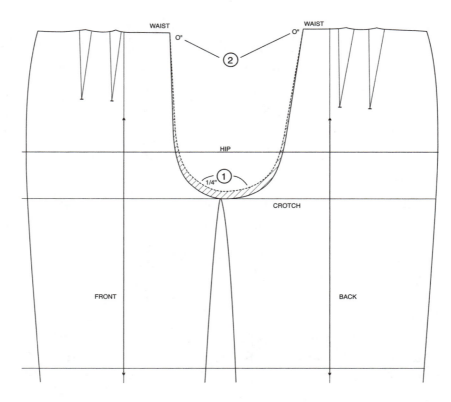

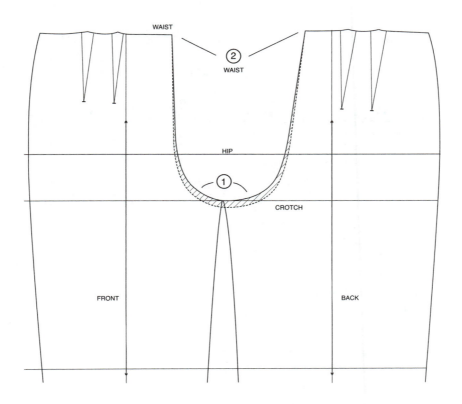

To tighten a loose crotch-front and back

1. Raise crotch curve desired amount.

2. Blend to 0" at waist.

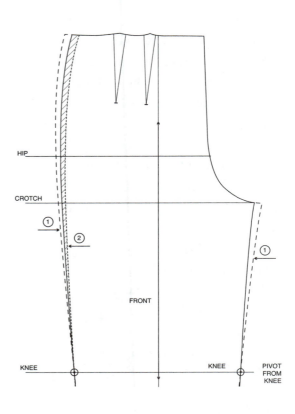

To increase or decrease fullness

1. Add length and fullness from crotch to knee.

   Add length fullness to side seam.

2. Decrease fullness at side seam.

   Keep length and fullness at crotch.

»

Chapter Five

Tracing, Cutting, and Testing Slopers

Objectives:

- Learn to trace adjusted slopers and sub-slopers to oak tag.
- Learn how to cut, test, pin, and fit your muslin on a form or body.

Trace Adjusted Slopers and Sub-Slopers to Oak Tag

Adjustments made on the slopers and sub-slopers should follow the rules used in making, correcting, and adjusting patterns. Rulers and curves must be used for precisely blending and connecting any new shapes. Patterns should be checked as follows:

- Check front and back shoulders and side seams for even measurements.
- Blend all waistline, neckline, and armholes using a curve.
- Use a ruler to redraw any straight lines.
- All darts, regardless of their size, are folded with the fullness of the dart towards the center front or center back, and the fold towards the side seams.
- True darts with curve or ruler depending on their position. (See the following figures.)

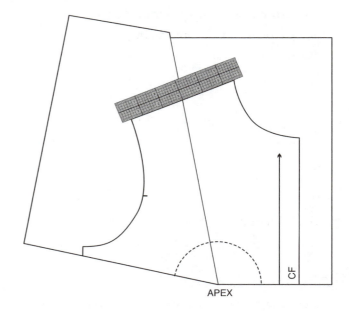

Bodice

Fold pattern horizontally across apex. This will enable easier folding of the shoulder dart. Then use ruler to redraw new straight shoulder line.

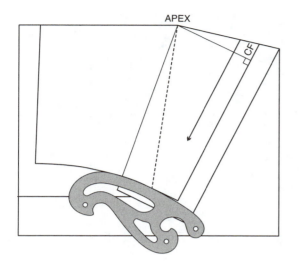

Bodice

Fold pattern horizontally across apex. This will enable easier folding of the waist dart. Fold sloper on dart lines and then use curve to blend and redraw waistline shape.

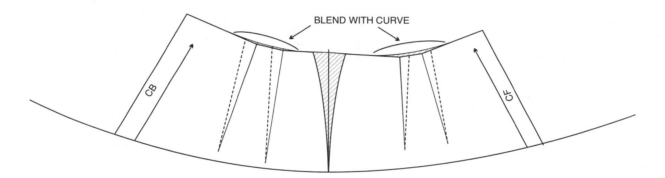

Skirts and Pants

Fold pattern at the point of each dart, front and back together. This will enable easier folding of the waist darts for a total waistline shape. Fold waist dart fullness towards center front and center back, then blend waistline with curve.

Cut Adjusted Slopers in Oak Tag

After slopers and sub-slopers are adjusted, corrected, trued, and checked for accuracy, they are then ready to be traced to oak tag and cut out. The method for tracing and trueing the oak tag can be applied to all slopers after adjusting.

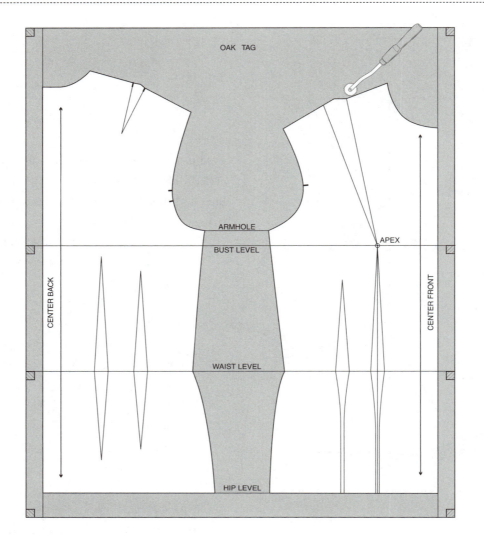

Front and Back Torso Sloper

1. Trace Sloper
   - On oak tag draw a vertical line parallel to the selvage of the front and back.
   - Square across oak tag with L-square at the bust, waist, and hip levels by measuring from bust, to waist, to hip; transfer these horizontal measurements to the oak tag.
   - Position front and back torso slopers with center front and center back against the vertically drawn lines.
   - Position the bust, waist, and hip levels on the horizontally drawn lines.
   - This process for positioning the slopers is to have side seams measuring and matching evenly.
   - Trace outline of sloper with a tracing wheel. Trace darts with a tracing wheel through the sloper.

2. Cut Sloper
   - Cut the Sloper out with a sharp paper scissors.
   - Using ruler and curve, redraw all the shapes and straight lines, as shown in the diagrams.

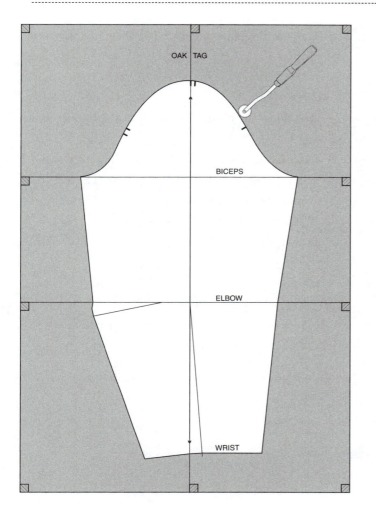

One-Dart Long Shaped Sleeve

1. Trace Sloper
   * Draw a vertical line through the center of the oak tag.
   * Measure from capline to biceps, to elbow. Square across horizontally from cut oak tag edges, as shown in diagram.
   * Allow several inches above capline and below wrist.
   * Position sleeve with with length grain over the vertically drawn line.
   * Position sleeve with the biceps and elbow lines of the sloper on the horizontally drawn lines.
   * Trace outline of sleeve.
2. Cut Sloper
   * Cut the sleeve sloper out repeating the steps outlined in step 2 on page 72.

* Slopers are usually drawn on oak tag without the seam allowance to develop new styles using the shape only. Seam allowances may get in the way of new pattern development and are usually added after the new style is completed. However, seam allowances can be added to slopers for testing and fitting.

Measure

1. Measure dress form or body and document all measurements on chart. Follow diagrams and instructions for measuring in chapter 2.

2. DO NOT CUT slopers out of the Pellon® sheets until all measurements are checked and compared to the measurements documented on the chart.

3. The Pellon® slopers can be traced to pattern paper and corrected and traced to the muslin for fitting. This would keep the Pellon® slopers intact for continued use.

Adjust

4. For minor adjustments see step 1, and step 2. The following two figures show how to adjust directly on the Pellon® sloper.

5. For all other adjustments follow diagrams shown in chapter 3.

Adding On

7. Add on to the bodice side seam as shown on page 75.

8. Extend side seams evenly from armhole to waist.

9. Add side seams back on to sloper. NOTE: Sleeve would also need to be adjusted the same amount on each side from biceps down to wrist. This is shown in chapter 3.

Cut

10. Cut Pellon® sloper out.

11. Pin together and test fit on form or body.

12. After test fitting the slopers can be cut in oak tag.

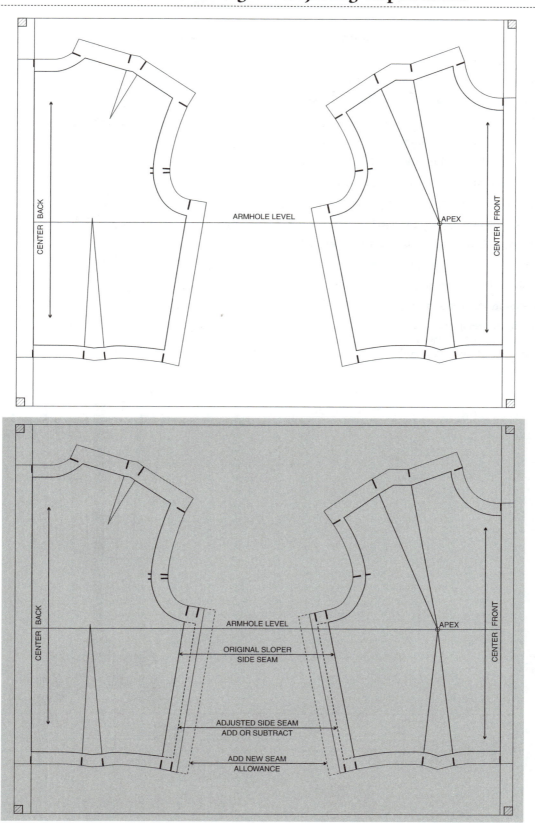

Test—Pin/Fit Your Muslin on a Form or Body

All slopers should be tested on the dress form or on the body. It is important to check for balance. All length grains should be perpendicular to the floor and all cross grains should be parallel to the floor. If the grain lines are not aligned properly, the garment will hang badly and will have pull lines in various areas.

When pinning the muslin, line up the cross grains, and pin up to the armhole on the bodice, or up to the waist on the skirt. Pin down to the waist on the bodice or down to the hem on the skirt. Keep the cross grain perpendicular and adjust and blend the armhole, waistline, and hemline if necessary.

All pins should be positioned perpendicular to the seams, as shown in the following three figures. Pin center front and center back on the form, as shown, for a test fit.

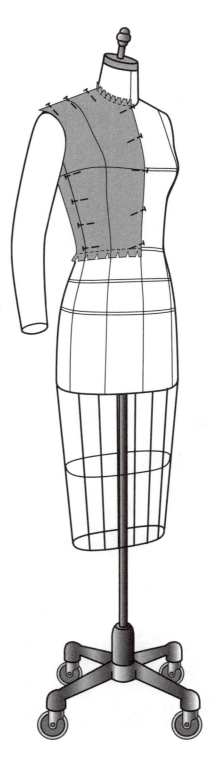

Muslin to Sloper #14 –
Princess bodice on dress form

Muslin to Sloper #2 –
2-dart straight skirt on dress form

Muslin to Slopers #4 and #8 –
Torso sloper on dress form and shaped,
1-dart sleeve on form

Chapter Six

Garment Lengths and Proportions

Objectives:
- Identify garment lengths of figures.
- Distinguish different types of fit.

Proportions–Garment Lengths on Figures

The measurements on the following figures show positions on the body for garment lengths. The measurements will vary depending on the height of the person.

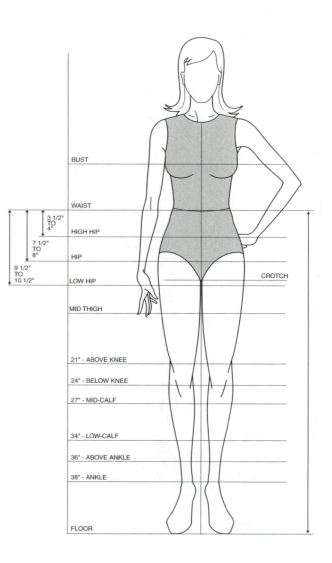

BUST

WAIST

3 1/2" TO 4"   HIGH HIP

7 1/2" TO 8"   HIP

9 1/2" TO 10 1/2"   LOW HIP   CROTCH

MID THIGH

21" - ABOVE KNEE

24" - BELOW KNEE

27" - MID-CALF

34" - LOW-CALF

36" - ABOVE ANKLE

38" - ANKLE

FLOOR

This figure shows proportions on a figure of average height. The measurements shown can be used for skirts and pants.

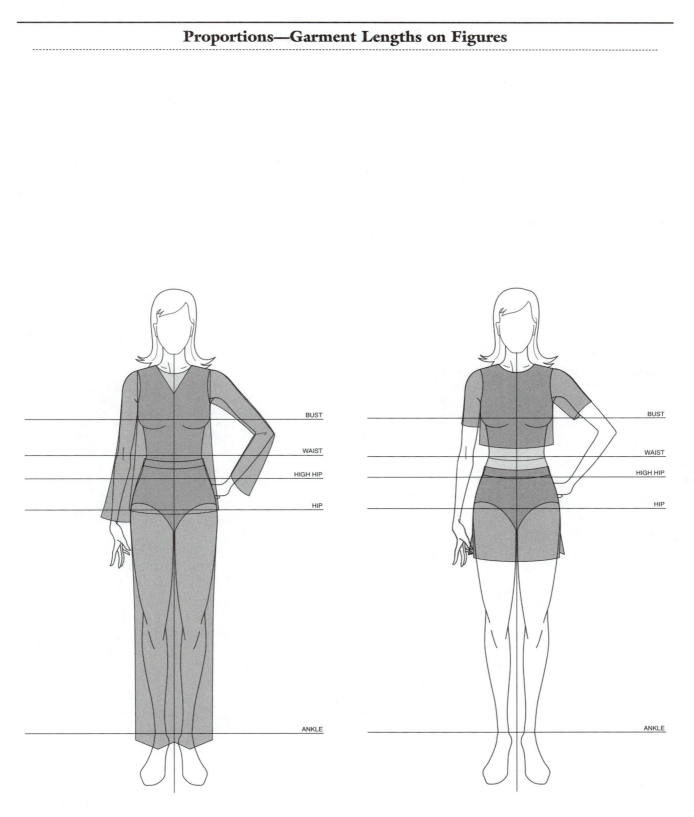

This figures shows straight-legged pant with waistband and bell sleeve, hip-length tunic over pant.

This figure shows dropped waistline mini-skirt, with side slits and shaped waistband along with short sleeve cropped top.

Different Types of Fit–
Garments Illustrated on Figures

The garments illustrated in the following figures fit
the body differently. After patterns are completed, the
style and fabric will determine the fit of the design.

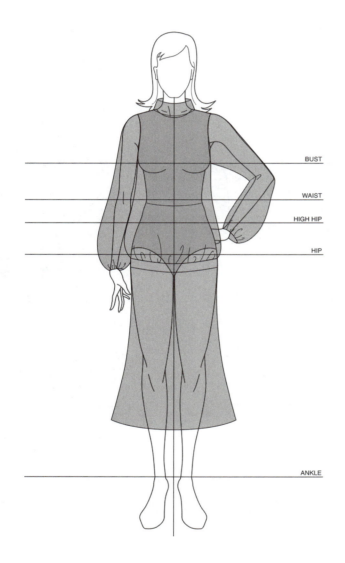

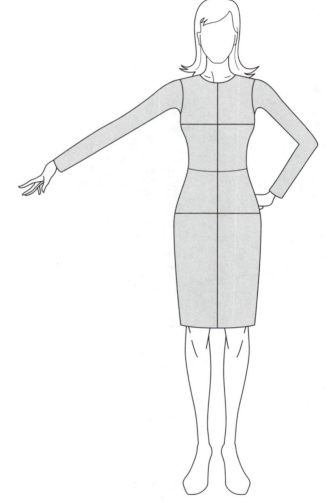

This figure shows midi-length (below calf) A-line dress,
with blouson hip length top gathered into band shaped
turtleneck collar, and full gathered long sleeves.

Tight Fit

This garment hugs the body and shows all curves.
Usually used for stretch fabrics.

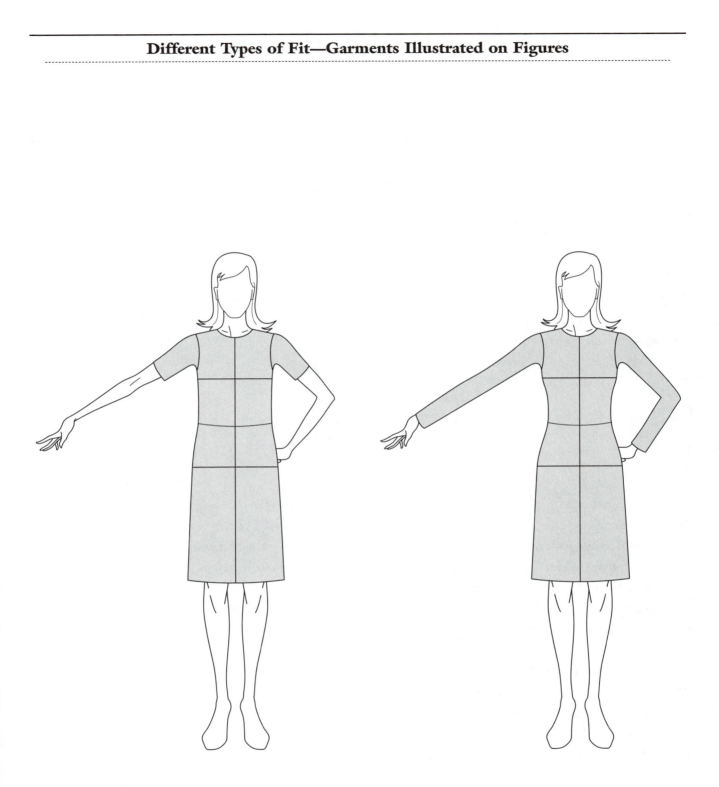

Semi-Fitted/Skimming the Hips
This is not as fitted as the Tight Fit garment, but skimming the hips.

Loose Fit/Slightly Dropped Shoulder
Garment hangs straight from the shoulders, skims the bust and hips. The dress also has a dropped armhole and slightly dropped shoulder. It is cut straight and with a minimum amount of A-Line shape at the hem.

Chapter Seven

Basic Grading

Objectives:

- Become familiar with a grading chart for sizing.
- Recognize diagrams for grading positions.

What Is Grading?

Grading is the method used in the design industry to increase or decrease patterns to fit the many size ranges of clothing. There are grading charts using specific measurements to increase or decrease the pattern.

Sample patterns used in industry for the missy size range are usually size 8. They are then graded down to the smallest size in the range and up to the largest size in the range that is used for a particular style and category. The grade between sizes increases in the larger sizes since larger bodies need more ease for comfortable movement. At the end of the chapter there are two charts that demonstrate pattern size and grading, including information for the full range of sizes.

Recommended book: *Professional Pattern Making for Designers: Women's Wear & Men's Casual Wear*, by Jack Handford, published by Fairchild Books.

Grading Measurements on Patterns Length and Width Grade

Patterns are graded horizontally and vertically in the precise positions shown in the following diagrams. Such precision maintains the line, balance, and proportion of the original sample size.

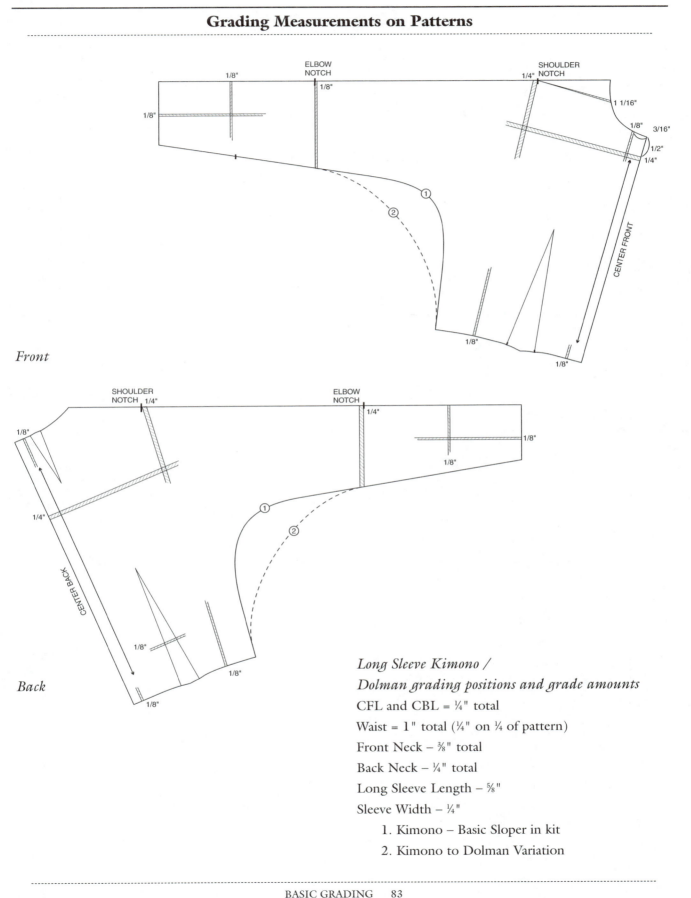

Front

Back

Long Sleeve Kimono /
Dolman grading positions and grade amounts

CFL and CBL = ¼" total

Waist = 1" total (¼" on ¼ of pattern)

Front Neck – ⅜" total

Back Neck – ¼" total

Long Sleeve Length – ⅝"

Sleeve Width – ¼"

1. Kimono – Basic Sloper in kit
2. Kimono to Dolman Variation

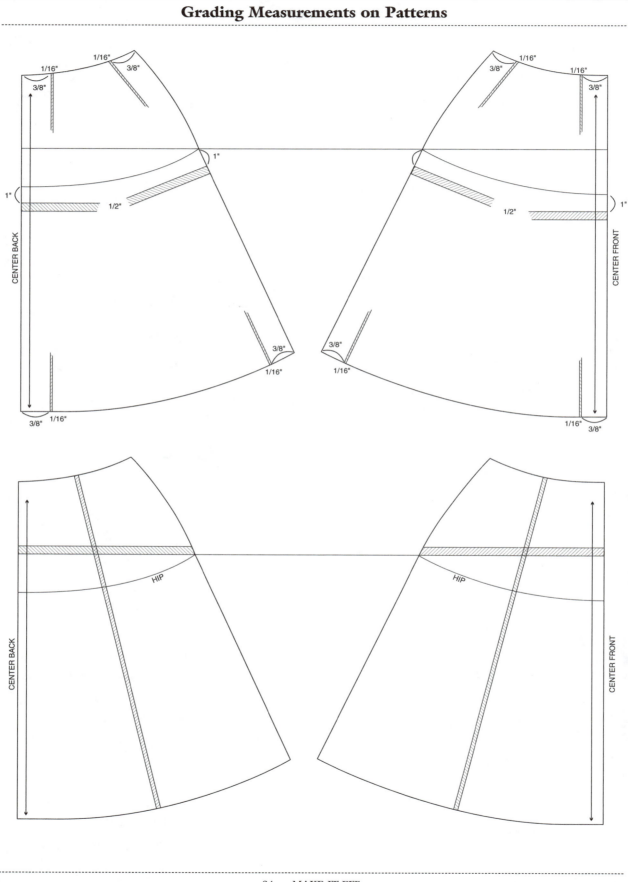

*Flared Skirt–Grading positions
and grade amounts*
Front and Back
CFL and CBL – ½" total
Waist – ½" total (⅛" on ¼" of pattern. This is a shaped
waistline.)
Hem Circumference – ½" total
≪

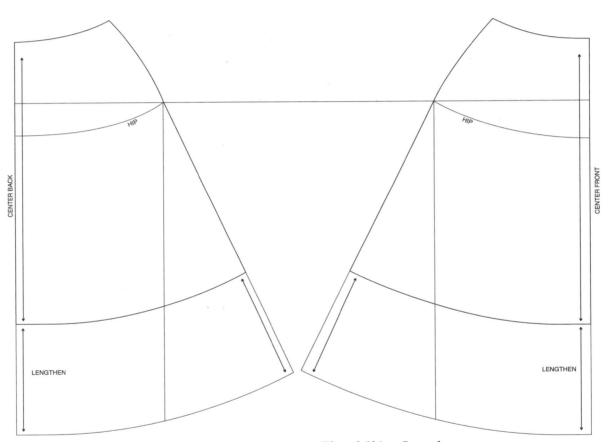

Flared Skirt–Lengthen
Front and Back
Extend CFL, CBL, and side seam to desired length.
This will widen the hem circumference proportionally.

*Flared Skirt—Grading and Fitting
by Slash and Spread; Mark and Shift*
Front and Back
CFL and CBL – desired amount necessary to fit
Waist and Hem – desired amount necessary for fit
≪

Grading Methods

Grading Patterns can be accomplished by several different methods.

1. Computer Grading: Used in industry by large manufacturing companies. Although the equipment is very expensive, this method is fast and accurate.
2. Table Grading Machine: This is a small movable machine that attaches to the edge of a cutting table. There are knobs that are turned and set to move the pattern in horizontal and vertical directions following preset measurements.
3. Cutting and Spreading: Patterns are cut and spread apart horizontally and vertically in the positions shown in the diagrams.

4. Shifting the Pattern: Patterns are moved up and down in the positions shown, by measuring and moving the pattern, outlining the sloper as it is moved to the right and left and up and down.

Patterns are graded evenly following the preestablished grading charts. However, patterns can be graded unevenly to accommodate body shapes. The bodice and individual skirt would need to be graded separately then put back together for a dress sloper.

The diagrams shown below establish the grading positions for slopers and patterns. By following the four grading methods, slopers and patterns can be increased or decreased.

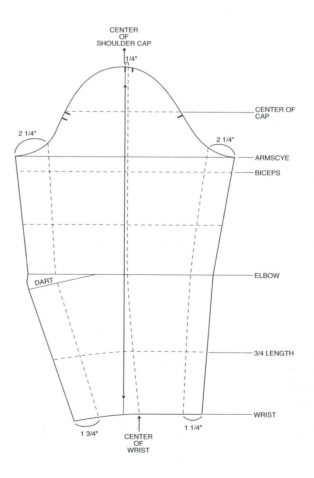

One-dart long sleeve

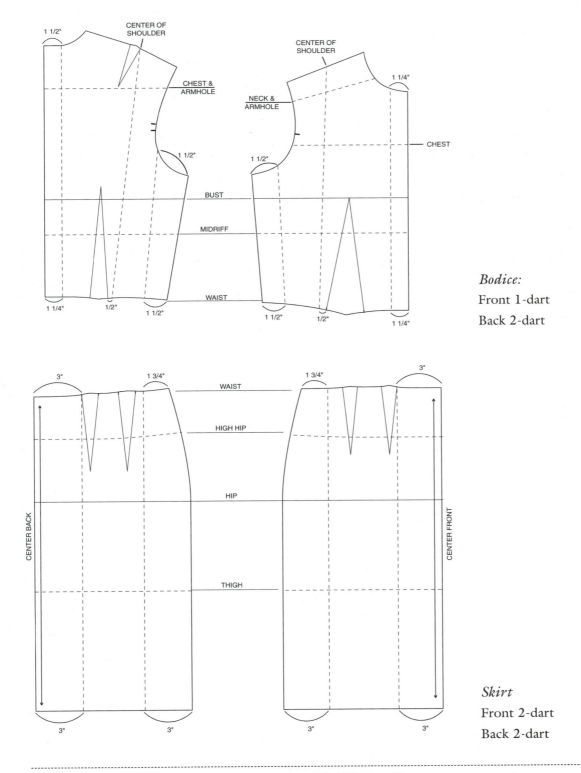

Bodice:

Front 1-dart

Back 2-dart

Skirt

Front 2-dart

Back 2-dart

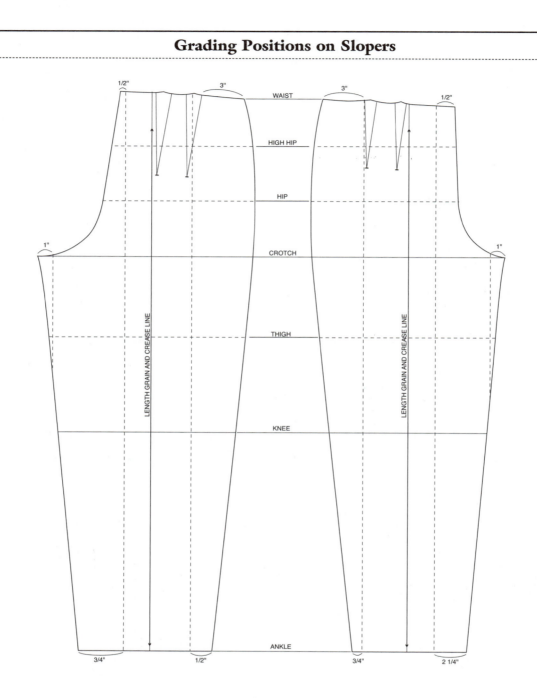

Pant

Front 2-dart

Back 2-dart

Front and Back Dress Form

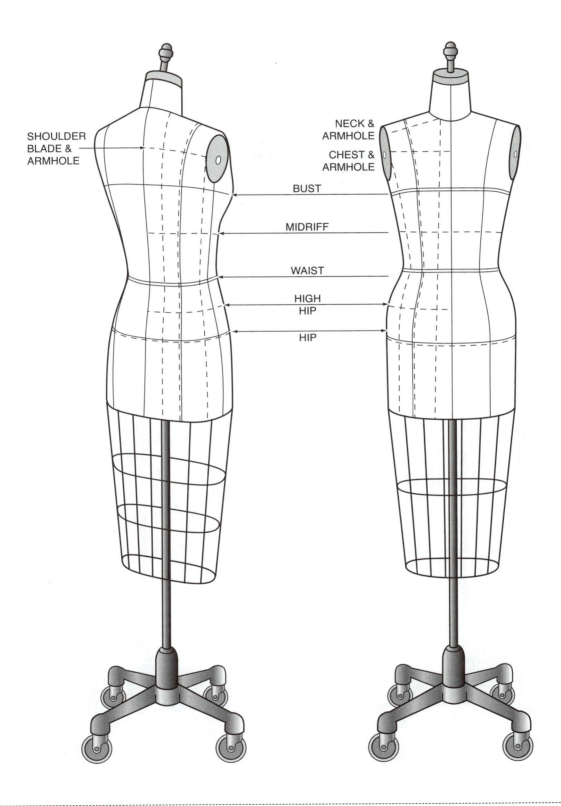

SHOULDER
BLADE &
ARMHOLE

NECK &
ARMHOLE

CHEST &
ARMHOLE

BUST

MIDRIFF

WAIST

HIGH
HIP

HIP

Front and Back Pant Form

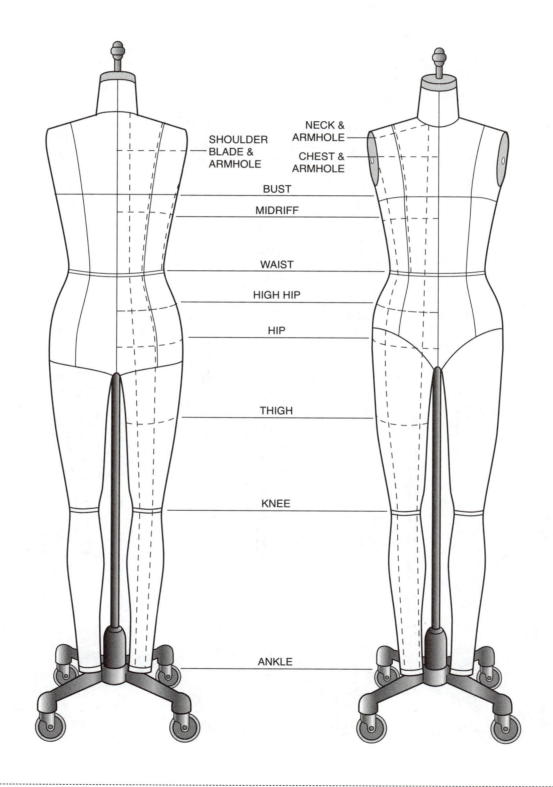

SHOULDER BLADE & ARMHOLE

NECK & ARMHOLE

CHEST & ARMHOLE

BUST

MIDRIFF

WAIST

HIGH HIP

HIP

THIGH

KNEE

ANKLE

Stuffed Arm

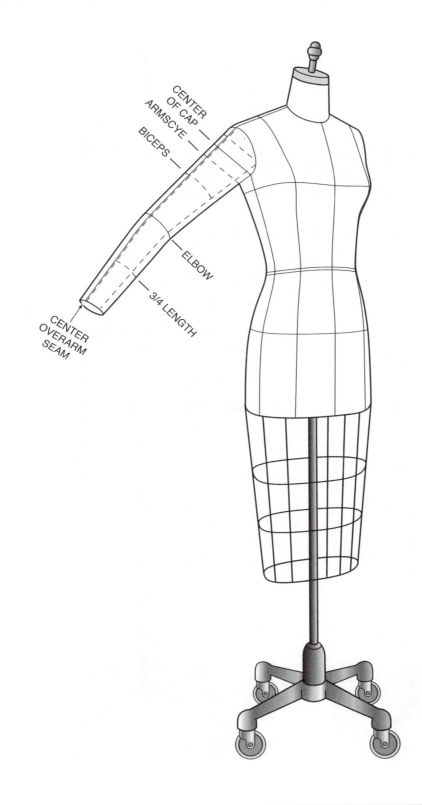

CENTER OF CAP

ARMSCYE

BICEPS

ELBOW

3/4 LENGTH

CENTER OVERARM SEAM

Front and Back Straight Fitted Dress

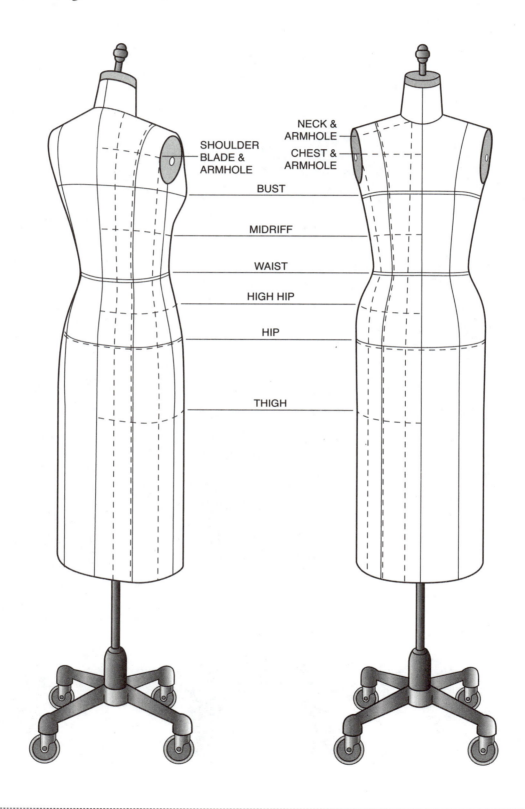

SHOULDER
BLADE &
ARMHOLE

NECK &
ARMHOLE

CHEST &
ARMHOLE

BUST

MIDRIFF

WAIST

HIGH HIP

HIP

THIGH

Pattern Size and Grading Charts

Table. 7.1
Pattern Size and Grading Chart

SIZE	4	6	8	10	12	14	16	18
BUST	32	33	34	35 ½	37	38 ½	40 ½	42 ½
WAIST	24	25	26	27 ½	29	30 ½	32 ½	34 ½
HIP	34	35	36	37 ½	39	40 ½	42 ½	44 ½

The above chart shows the basic size grade between sizes 4–8 which is 1" between sizes. The grade shown between sizes 10–14 is 1 ½" between sizes. The grade shown between sizes 14–18 is 2" between sizes.
NOTE: Measurements on grading and size charts vary according to manufacturer and their established fit. They are based on government specifications.

Table 7.2
Wolf Form Co. Missy Dress Sizes

	XS	S	S	M	M	L	L	XL
FRENCH	34	36	38	40	42	44	46	48
SIZE	4	6	8	10	12	14	16	18
CHEST	32	33	34	35	36 ½	38	39 ½	41
BUST	32 ½	33 ½	34 ½	35 ½	37	38 ½	40	41 ½
WAIST	23	24	25	26	27 ½	29	30 ½	32
HIPS @ 4" High Hip	31 ¼	32 ¼	33 ¼	34 ¼	35 ¾	37 ¼	38 ¾	40 ½
HIPS @ 8" + or - ¼"	34	35	36	37	38 ½	40	41 ½	43
CENTER BACK LENGTH	16 ¼	16 ½	16 ¾	17	17 ¼	17 ½	17 ¾	18
CENTER FRONT LENGTH	13 ¾	14	14 ¼	14 ½	14 ¾	15	15 ¼	15 ½
ACROSS SHOULDER	14 ¼	14 ½	14 ¾	15	15 ⅜	15 ¾	16 ⅛	16 ½
ACROSS BACK–4" below neck	13 ½	13 ¾	14	14 ¼	14 ⅝	15	15 ⅜	15 ¾
DIAPHRAGM–under bust	27	28	29	30	31 ½	33	34 ½	36
DIAPHRAGM–midway	25 ½	26 ½	27 ½	28 ½	30	31 ½	33	34 ½
SHOULDER–neck to shoulder bone	4 ¾	4 ⅞	5	5 ⅛	5 ¼	5 ⅜	5 ½	5 ⅝
NECK	12 ¾	13 ¼	13 ¾	14 ¼	14 ¾	15 ¼	15 ¾	16 ¼

Table 7.2 continued
Wolf Form Co. Missy Dress Sizes

	XS	S	S	M	M	L	L	XL
BUST–around neck for HALTER	24	24 ¾	25 ¼	26 ¼	27	27 ¾	28 ½	29 ½
ACROSS BUST + or -⅛"	6 ¾	7	7 ¼	7 ½	7 ¾	8	8 ¼	8 ½
ACROSS CHEST–1 ½" below neck	12 ½	12 ¾	13	13 ¼	13 ⅝	14	14 ⅜	14 ¾
BNS–back neck to shoulder seam + or - ⅛"	2 ⅝	2 ¾	2 ⅞	3	3 ⅛	3 ¼	3 ⅜	3 ½
CERVICAL HEIGHT–stature	55	55 ½	56	56 ½	57	57 ½	58	58 ½
HEAD–height	8 ¼	8 ½	8 ¾	9	9 ¼	9 ½	9 ¾	10
HEAD–circumference	20 ½	21	21 ½	22	22 ½	23	23 ½	24
WAIST to FLOOR	39	39 ⅜	39 ¾	40 ⅛	40 ½	40 ⅞	42 ¼	41 ⅝
CROTCH W.W. {FR. 10–12 ¾"} {BK. 13 ½"}	24	24 ¾	25 ½	26 ¼	27	27 ¾	28 ½	29 ¼
TRUE RISE	9 ¼	9 ½	9 ¾	10	10 ¼	10 ½	10 ¾	11 ¼
CROTCH–height	29 ½	29 ⅝	39 ¾	30	30 ⅛	30 ¼	30 ⅜	30 ½
MAXIMUM–thigh	19 ¼	20	20 ¾	21 ½	22 ½	23 ½	24 ½	25 ½
MIDDLE–thigh	17	17 ½	18	18 ½	19 ¼	20	20 ¾	21 ½
KNEE	12 ⅞	13 ¼	13 ⅝	14	14 ½	15	15 ½	16
KNEE–height	18	18 ¼	18 ½	18 ⅜	18 ½	18 ⅝	18 ¾	18 ⅞
ANKLE	9 ¼	9 ½	9 ¾	10	10 ¼	10 ½	10 ¾	11
ANKLE–length	2 ¾	2 ¾	2 ¾	2 ¾	2 ¾	2 ¾	2 ¾	2 ¾
CALF	11 ⅞	12 ¼	12 ⅝	13	13 ½	14	14 ½	15

Missy Arm Measurements

SIZE	4	6	8	10	12	14	16	18
TORSO – VERTICAL TRUNK	55	56 ¼	57 ½	58 ¾	60	61 ¼	62 ½	63 ¾
	57 ¼	58 ½	59 ¾	61	63 ¼	63 ½	64 ¾	66
ARMSCYE	13 ⅝	14	14 ⅜	14 ¾	15 ⅛	15 ½	15 ⅞	16 ¼
UPPER ARM	10 ¼	10 ½	10 ¾	11	11 ⅜	11 ¾	12 ⅛	12 ¾
ELBOW	9 ½	9 ⅝	9 ¾	9 ⅞	10 ⅛	10 ⅜	10 ⅝	11
WRIST	5 ¾	5 ⅞	6	6 ⅛	6 ¼	6 ⅜	6 ½	6 ⅝
ARM LENGTH – shoulder bone to wrist	23 ⅛	24	23 ½	23 ⅔	23 ⅞	24 1/16	24 ¼	24 7/15
ARM LENGTH – shoulder to elbow	13 ⅜	13 ½	13 ⅝	13 ¾	13 ⅞	14	14 ⅛	14 ¼
ARM LENGTH – CBN to wrist	30 ⅛	30 ¾	31 1/16	31 ⅝	31 ¾	32 ⅛	32 ½	32 15/16
SCYE DEPTH	7 ¼	7 ⅜	7 ½	7 ⅝	7 ¾	7 ⅞	8	8 ⅛
NECK TO BUST POINT	9 ½	9 ¾	10	10 ¼	10 ⅝	11	11 ⅜	11 ⅞

Chapter Eight

Converting Basic Slopers to Knit Slopers

Objectives:

- Identify and follow instructions for converting basic slopers on knit fabrics.

The following four illustrations show the slopers for a basic torso, sleeve, skirt, and pant.

The illustrations are shown as basic slopers, from the *Make It Fit* sloper kit and are converted to basic knit slopers, in three steps.

The knit slopers are used in the same way as for woven fabrics. Knit fabrics do not all have the same stretch properties, so the patterns are then adjusted for fit, depending on the amount of stretch and memory for each knit.

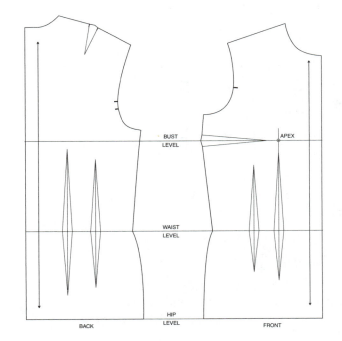

Step 1 Converting woven torso slopers to knit slopers

1. Trace front and back torso slopers.
2. Trace length and cross grains.
3. Trace darts and armhole notches.

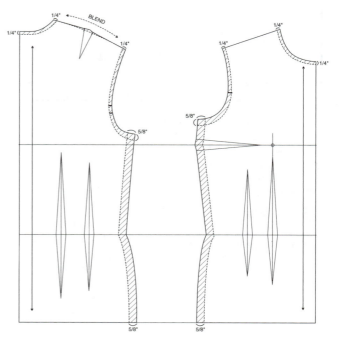

Step 2

1. Blend off shoulder dart, slightly rounding shoulder line.
2. Decrease width at armhold ¼" at shoulder, dropping to ⅝" at armhole.
3. Decrease width of body ⅝" from armhole to hip.

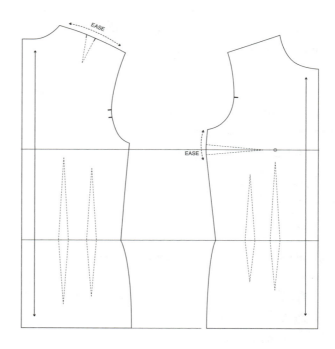

Completed knit torso slopers

1. Back shoulder and front bust darts are eased into seamlines at shoulder and side seams.
2. Slopers show position of eliminated darts.

Converting Woven Sleeve Slopers to Knit Slopers

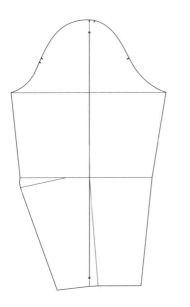

Step 1 Converting woven sleeve sloper to knit sleeve sloper

1. Trace long shaped one-dart sleeve.

2. Trace length and cross grains.

3. Trace dart and cap notches.

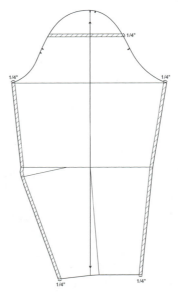

Step 2

1. Decrease width at underarm seam ¼".

2. Shorten cap ¼" by overlapping and reblending cap shape.

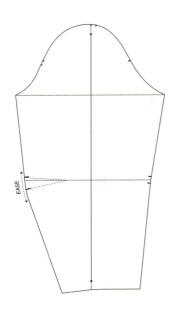

Completed knit sleeve sloper

1. Dart is eased in at elbow from back to front under-arm seam.

2. Sloper shows position of eliminated dart.

Converting Woven Skirt Slopers to Knit Slopers

Step 1 Trace basic one-dart sloper.

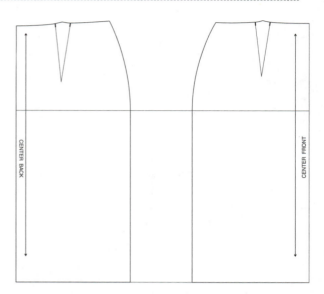

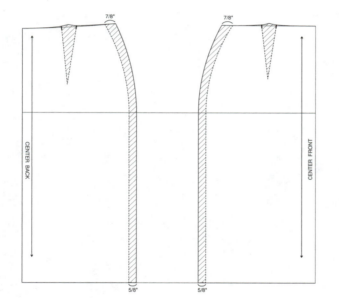

Step 2 Convert basic skirt sloper to knit sloper.

1. Eliminate darts.
2. Tighten side seams as illustrated.

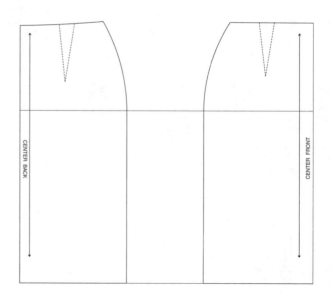

Completed basic knit skirt sloper.

Converting Woven Pant Slopers to Knit Slopers

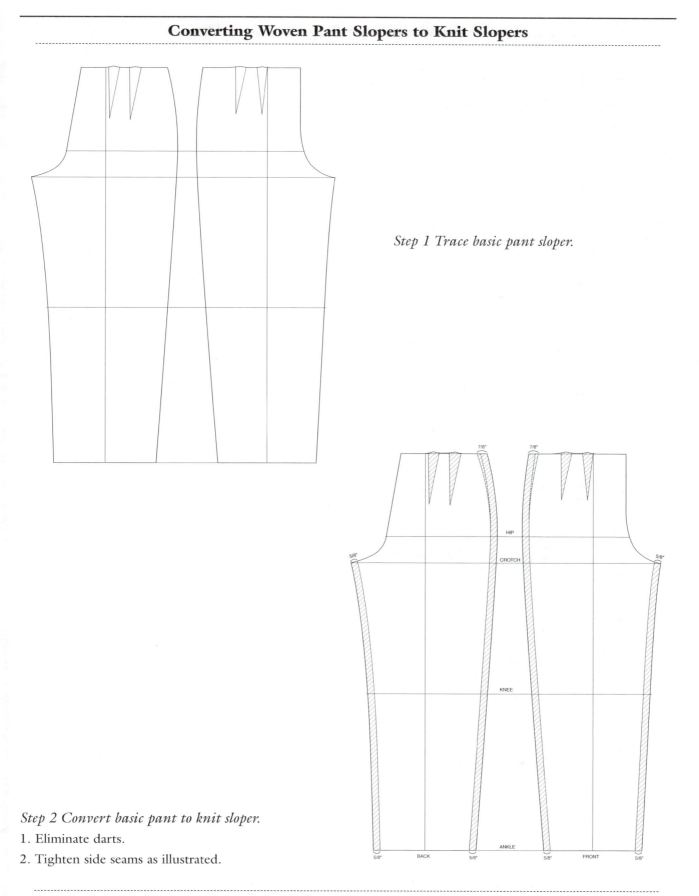

Step 1 Trace basic pant sloper.

Step 2 Convert basic pant to knit sloper.

1. Eliminate darts.

2. Tighten side seams as illustrated.

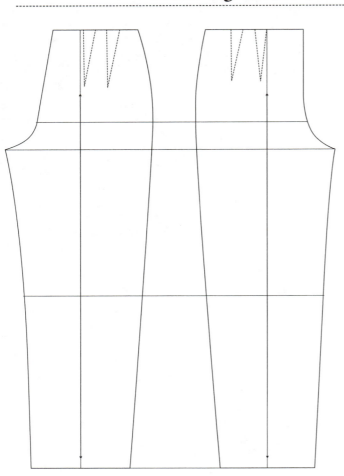

Completed basic knit pant sloper.

Chapter Nine

Scaling Slopers

Objectives:

- Learn the meaning of scaling slopers.
- Learn methods for scaling patterns for bodices, skirts, sleeves, and pants.

Scaling patterns and slopers is a method of taking a pattern to a larger size, as illustrated in this chapter. Scaling can be used to scale a pattern fully or partially in specific areas.

Any ¼" or ½" scale sloper or pattern can become a full size pattern by measuring and doubling the ½" scale sloper or pattern.

Patterns or slopers can be scaled up from ¼" size to ½" size and then to a full size pattern. Any pattern or design that is developed using ¼" or ½" slopers can be scaled to full size, cut, and test fitted in muslin. The full size slopers in the *Make It Fit* pattern kit can be scaled to larger sizes, using the method shown. It is important to measure accurately and extend the A, B, C, etc. measuring points precisely. Connect all the points, using a curve for the neckline, armhole, waistline, and hiplines; use a ruler for shoulder seams and darts.

Front and back bodice slopers should be traced and the darts marked. All the scale lines for enlarging the pattern are marked from the apex point of the bust dart on the bodice.

The scale lines on the torso sloper are drawn from the apex point of the bust dart, and the top of the waist dart, which touches the apex point.

The scale lines for the sleeve sloper are drawn from the center of the cap on the biceps, by dividing the sleeve cap as illustrated on pages 104 and 105. The scale lines for the pant extend from the point of the waist dart.

Connect all the new points to form the new pattern outline. Shape, blend, and draw lines using a ruler and curves.

Use: Front and back bodice and sleeves as a guide for scaling all patterns (see pages 102–105).

One-dart Front Bodice

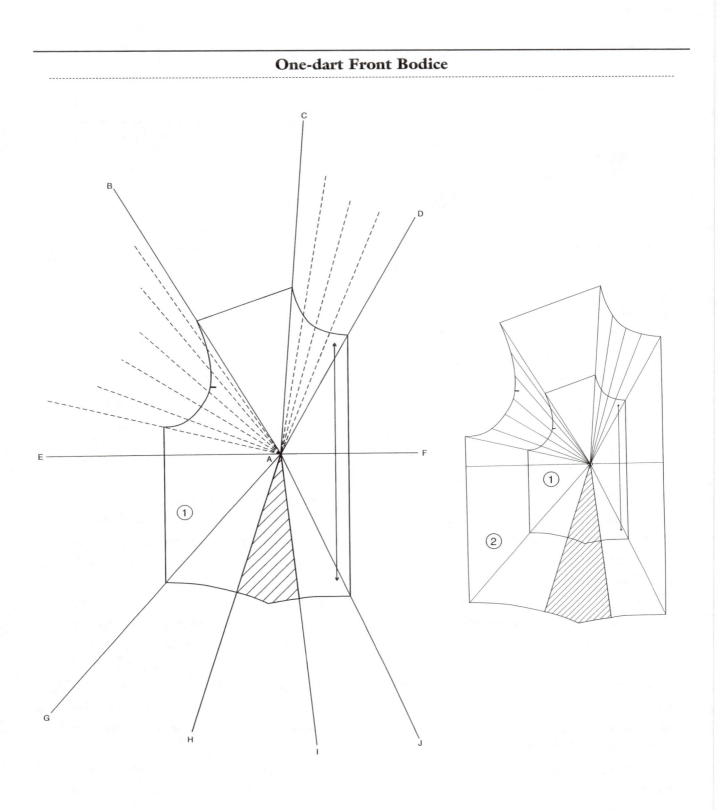

1. Measure and extend lines as shown for front bodice.

2. Completed pattern after scaling (shown in smaller size).

Two-dart Back Bodice

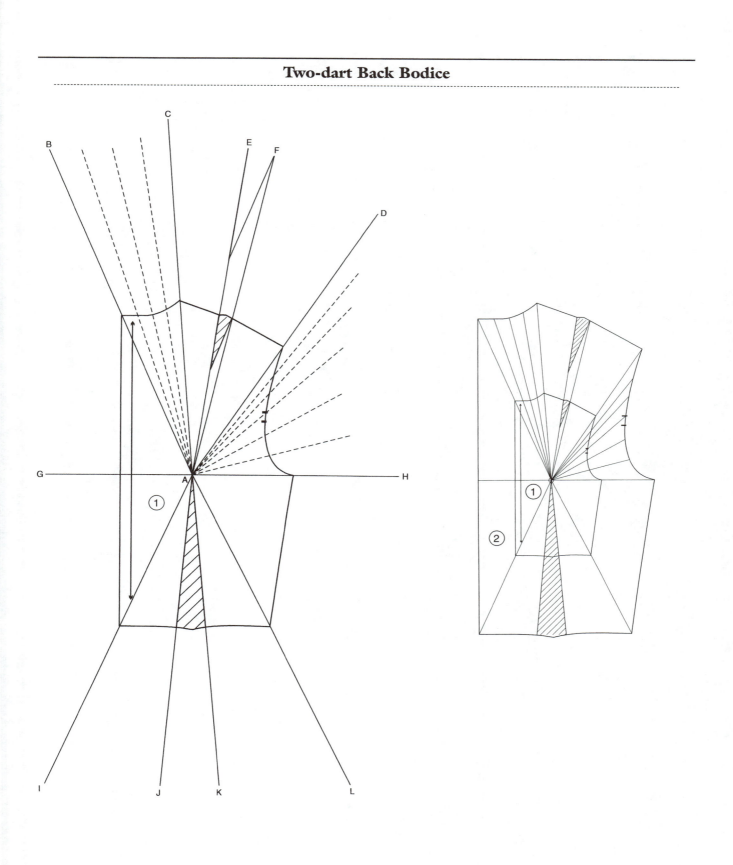

1. Measure and extend lines as shown for back bodice.

2. Completed pattern after scaling (shown in smaller size).

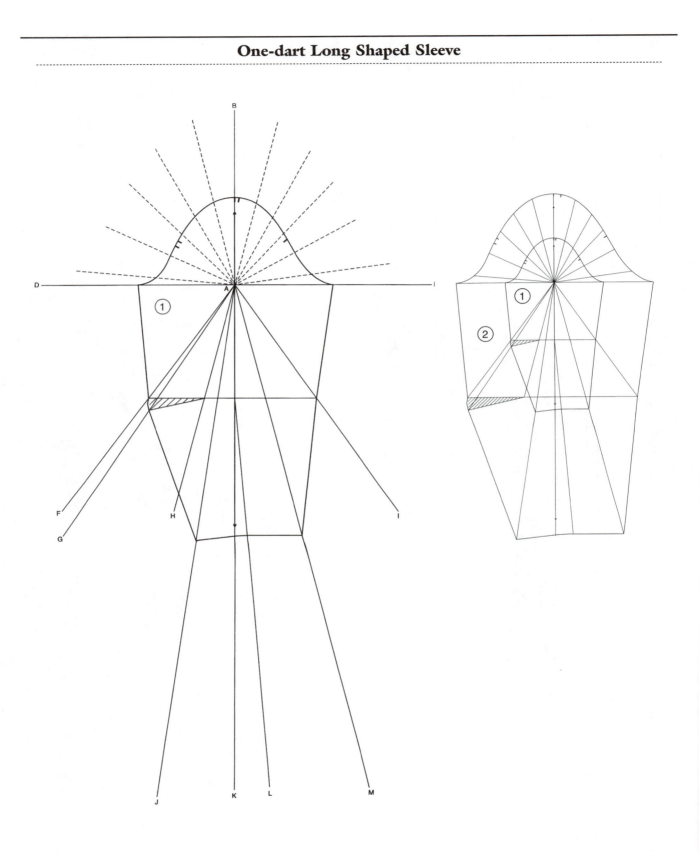

1. Measure and extend lines as shown for one-dart shaped sleeve.

2. Completed pattern after scaling (shown in smaller size).

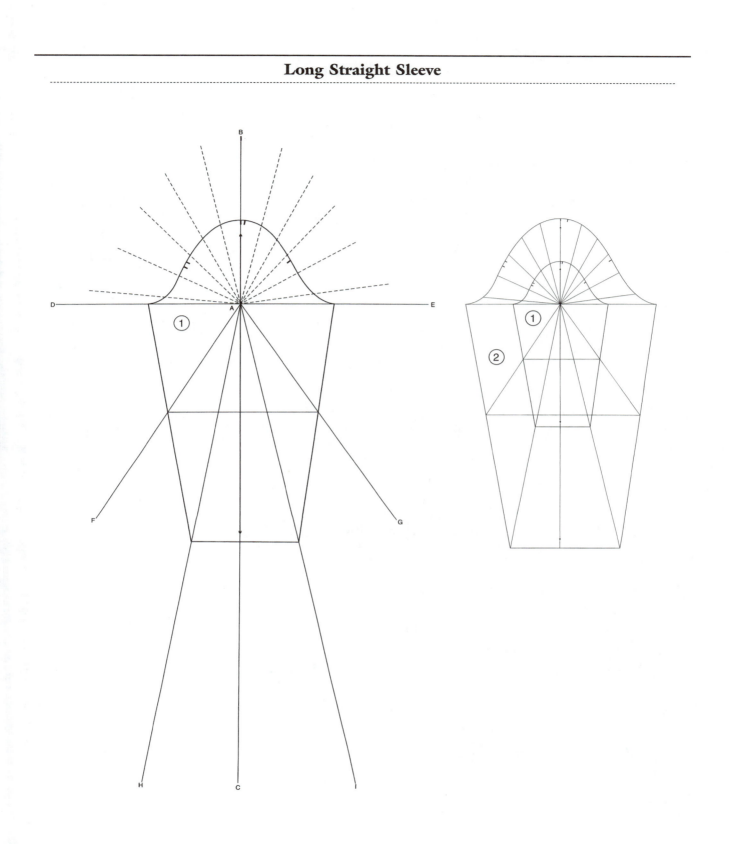

1. Measure and extend lines as shown for straight sleeve.

2. Completed pattern after scaling (shown in smaller size).

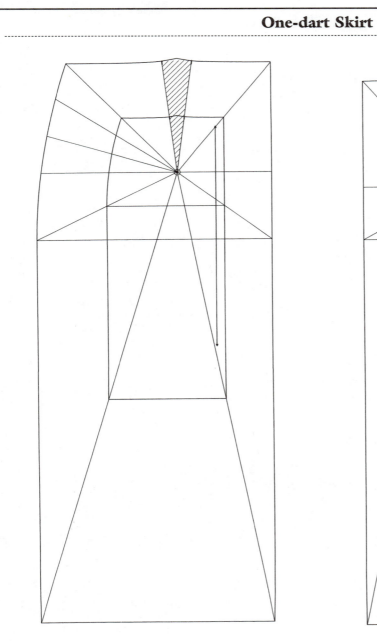

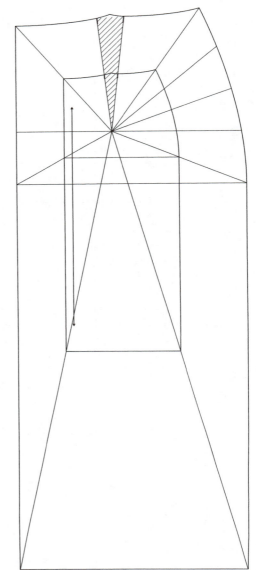

Front   *Back*

Completed skirt after patterns are scaled.

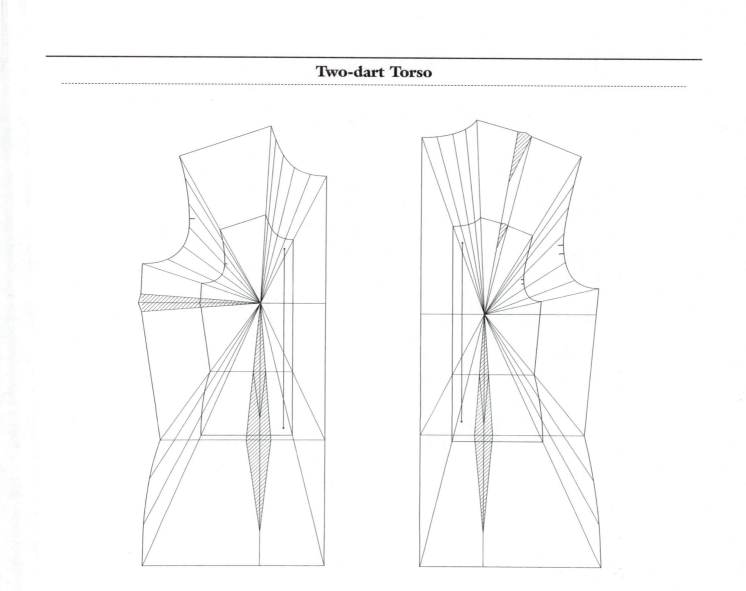

Front   *Back*

Completed skirt after patterns are scaled.

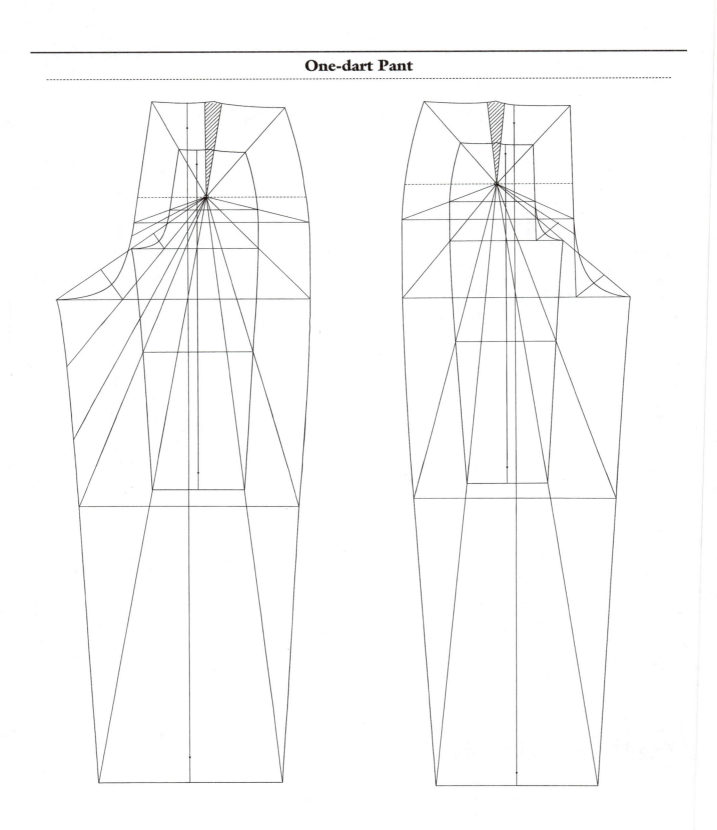

Front

Back

Completed pant after patterns are scaled.